THE SEVENTH SHOT

by Ann Burke

Library and Archives Canada Cataloguing in Publication

Title: The seventh shot / by Ann Burke.
Other titles: 7th shot
Names: Burke, Ann, 1947- author.
Identifiers: Canadiana (print) 20200284495 | Canadiana (ebook) 2020028455X |
ISBN 9781988989235
    (softcover) | ISBN 9781988989310 (EPUB)
Subjects: LCSH: West, Ronald Glen. | LCSH: Murderers—Ontario—Biography. |
LCSH: Rapists—Ontario—
    Biography. | LCSH: Thieves—Ontario—Biography. | LCSH: Ex-police officers—
Ontario—Biography. |
    LCGFT: Biographies.
Classification: LCC HV6248.W47 B87 2020 | DDC 364.152/3092—dc23

Book Design: Heather Campbell
Edited by: Mitchell Gauvin

Printed and bound in Canada on 100% recycled paper.

Published by:
Latitude 46 Publishing
info@latitude46publishing.com
Latitude46publishing.com

The production of this book was made possible through the generous assistance of the Ontario Arts Council.

ONTARIO ARTS COUNCIL
CONSEIL DES ARTS DE L'ONTARIO
an Ontario government agency
un organisme du gouvernement de l'Ontario

THE SEVENTH SHOT

by Ann Burke

TABLE OF CONTENTS

ACKNOWLEDGMENTS

I wish to thank all those who kindly shared some of the best and worst moments of their lives with me; for some, a gratifying experience, and for others, most painful.

Thanks to those who worked diligently to unearth old records, as well as to those who reminded me that, even in very dark moments, it is okay to smile and laugh.

My greatest thanks to my home team: Team Burke. To my husband, Gordon, for putting up with me when the creative well ran dry. To Jennifer Bennett, my daughter, and Patrick Bennett, my son-in-law, for their enthusiastic encouragement and much needed technical support. To Kelly Noussis, my dear "Dils" (daughter-in-law), for dragging me, kicking and screaming, into the world of websites, blogging, podcasts, and the other stuff she continues to work on.

Ultimately, many thanks to the person without whose editorial guidance, direction, coaxing, and input, *The Seventh Shot* would have remained just an idea—my son, Matt Burke.

*Dedicated to those who wait for justice
and to those who seek to bring it.*

CHAPTER ONE

Murder in the Moraine

"Murderers are not monsters, they're men. And that's the most frightening thing about them."

—**Alice Sebold**, *The Lovely Bones*

At six foot one and 130 pounds, Don Hillock was what some would describe as "a tall drink of water." After being turned away by both the Royal Canadian Mounted Police and the Ontario Provincial Police with the suggestion he come back when he'd put on at least thirty additional pounds, Don heard that the police department of Whitchurch—which would become a part of York Regional Police in 1971—was looking for a cadet in Aurora.

"I didn't have a clue where Aurora was," said Don. So began the first-hand recollection of things I had only read about in old archives. Don and his wife Joan had welcomed me into their home in Orangeville, Ontario. Joan and I sat silently at the kitchen table as Don stirred a huge pot of chili and enthusiastically recounted the events as if they had occurred yesterday.

Hillock, who hailed from Alton in Caledon Township, was fortunate they didn't give a damn how much he weighed. On October 28, 1960, the nineteen-year-old would begin his career as a cadet. Little did anyone know that eventually he would not only serve as chief of police for the region, but that the future York Region Police headquarters would be established on Don Hillock Drive in Aurora. We laughed about the fact that it was considerably easier to Google and find Don Hillock Drive than it was to track down Don Hillock himself.

However, those achievements were still far off in the future when—nearly a decade into Don's career—the now-Sergeant Hillock was to arrive at a horrific crime scene. May 6, 1970 was to remain vivid in his recollections nearly fifty years later. I sat back, almost breathless, poised to hear from the person who had witnessed the initial nightmarish crime first-hand. I could finally put meat on the bones of fifty-year-old archival records and newspaper clippings.

The beautiful and distinct Oak Ridges Moraine of Southern Ontario extends 160 kilometres from the Niagara Escarpment in the west to the Trent River system in the east and covers nineteen hundred square kilometres, extending in a line that seemingly dogs Lake Ontario. Mixed forest, bogs, tail grass, prairie, and oak savannah woodlands dot the region, collectively supporting a habitat for a wide array of unique flora and fauna.

The little hamlet of Gormley sits nestled amongst the ridges of the moraine, at one time straddling the townships of Markham to the south and Whitchurch to the north, later to be divided by Highway 404. Once the home of the Cement Block and Tile Company, Gormley stood conveniently placed for access to the CNR rail immediately to the west. In 1970, Gormley remained a largely rural area, far from the clamour of city life, yet close enough for commuting. It was an idyllic setting and to this day remains relatively protected by its placement within the Moraine.

It was during this time that a young couple, Doreen and Albert Moorby, resided in Gormley with their twenty-one-month-old son, Brent. They had moved to the area in 1961 and now lived on the Bethesda Side Road in a small but attractive modern A-frame home. The house sat back from the road, only partially concealed by a small row of fir trees.

The weather in the area in May of 1970 was exceptional, with temperatures ranging from a frigid 2° Celsius to a positively balmy 29°. Wednesday, May 6, was bright but cool, and dawned early like most other mornings for parents of a toddler. At 7:45 a.m., Albert left in the family's '68 Chevy Camaro—typically leaving the garage door up—as he departed for his teaching position at Donhead Secondary, where he taught physical education. Prior to Brent's birth, Doreen June Moorby had practiced as a Canadian Mothercraft nurse, training to assist in the development of healthy babies. For the meantime, with young Brent to care for, she had chosen to stay home and give the toddler her full attention, still putting her chosen profession to good use.

On this lovely spring day there was no indication that the events to follow would irrevocably alter the lives of those involved forever. In fact, exactly what did occur and who was responsible would remain a troubling mystery for nearly thirty years.

—**Moorby Residence. (Ontario Archives)**

Albert Moorby returned home at 5:40 p.m., looking forward to another pleasant evening with his little family. After pulling up to the house, he was surprised to find the front door locked. This was decidedly unusual. After retrieving the spare key from the garage, he gained entry to the house.

His first recollection was of hearing Brent sobbing weakly from the kitchen at the rear of the house. As he proceeded towards the crying, he was met with an absolutely horrific sight: Doreen lying face-down in a pool of blood, with Brent partially pinned beneath her legs. Albert's immediate impression was that Doreen may have fallen and hit her head on the corner of the table. There was just so much blood. Dropping to his knees, Albert found Doreen to be cold to the touch. He quickly pulled the sobbing, blood-smeared toddler from beneath his mother. It was later established that Brent had been trapped beneath his mother's legs for some time as suggested by the pressure marks noted on his lower limbs. Otherwise he remained uninjured.

Overcome with shock, Albert still had the mindfulness to grab Brent and dart with him, feet barely touching the ground, to the home of an elderly couple who lived about two hundred yards to the west of the Moorby residence.

At 5:45 p.m., using the neighbours' phone, Albert called the Whitchurch Police Department and spoke with Constable Dennis Prop. The constable urged Moorby to return and do mouth-to-mouth resuscitation on Doreen. Leaving Brent with the neighbours, Albert returned to the house and Doreen, turning her over and commencing mouth-to-mouth.

Sergeant Don Hillock, now of the Whitchurch Police, was the first officer on the scene, arriving at 5:53 p.m. Hillock, along with an OPP investigator and a fire marshal, had been on his way to interview the local town clerk in relation to a fire in the town's vault.

"There had been no response from the uniform car to Mr. Moorby's call," Hillock later recounted. "I had said, 'Okay, I'll go down there then.' It was a total coincidence that I ended up there that day. When I arrived, I found Mr. Moorby right out of it and I don't blame him at all. He was screaming hysterically and his face and mouth were grotesquely covered in blood from attempting to resuscitate Doreen. I had to deal with him first. Mr. Moorby shortly left for Doreen's sister's home in Unionville, taking the infant with him. When I went inside and surveyed the scene, I immediately found it hard to see how it was possible that Mrs. Moorby had received that much damage just from a fall, as first suggested."

Hillock found Doreen on her back in the doorway to the ground-floor bedroom, with her feet pointing towards the bedroom and her head towards the kitchen. She was wearing slacks and a flowered blouse, as well as a pair of slippers. The front of Doreen's blouse was open and blood-stained. He found no pulse in her neck or arm. "Her right arm was cold and her lips and chin bluish." Hillock applied a resuscitator and attempted heart massage, but with no response.

"I had immediately gotten on the radio to get a coroner to the scene," said Hillock, but it was after 6:30 p.m. when Dr. A. W. Diamond of Aurora, summoned by Markham, arrived with Staff Sergeant David Fellows of the Whitchurch Township Police. Immediately after he arrived, a general practitioner, Dr. D.H. Smith of Stouffville, showed up, being called out by the Whitchurch Police Detachment.

Diamond examined the body briefly, suggesting that death had most likely resulted from a fall causing Doreen's head to come in contact with something hard, such as the natural tile floor or table corner. Rigor mortis was noticeable in her facial muscles, jaw, neck, and upper arms. The coroner would determine time of death to be between two and four hours prior to examination, putting it between 2:30 and 4:30 p.m. A witness's testimony would later suggest that it may have been earlier—in fact, prior to 1:50 p.m.

Don shook his head as he later reflected on the events engraved in his memory. It made no sense to him that the coroner hadn't even turned the body over: "If they had, they would have seen the gun shots!"

The other injuries—and there were a number of them—were not immediately apparent, due to the huge blood loss and the fact that Doreen had been flipped over onto her back by Albert to begin resuscitation. Had the coroner turned the body back over, it is highly probable that he would have seen the defence wounds where bullets had pierced Doreen's hands, as well as the bullet holes in Doreen's blouse. He also may have noticed the gun shots to her head in spite of the blood-matted hair. The coroner scheduled an autopsy for the following day at 10:00 a.m. Nobody was talking murder at this point—after all, there were no cartridges and no signs of a struggle.

By 8:00 p.m. that evening, the OPP had arrived on site and a series of photographs were taken. By 8:30 p.m. the body was removed. Sergeant Hillock and Constable Bryan Cousineau of Whitchurch would spend the night at the residence as they waited for their chief to confirm that the OPP would take the lead. "We drew sketches and detailed the crime scene overnight," said Hillock, who had the foresight to take all the precautions needed if the home was to be considered a crime scene. "We had coffee delivered at some point and were careful not to contaminate the scene. I continued to feel conflicted about the amount of blood attributed to a fall against a table corner. She did not hit her head on a table corner. I thought this from minute one. There was too much blood, for one thing. I've seen a lot of accidents and murder scenes and it just didn't add up," Don stated emphatically.

Don Hillock would attend with the body at the Newmarket Hospital morgue. His suspicions were to soon be confirmed: During the examination at York County Hospital, upon removal of Doreen's blouse to facilitate x-rays, it was revealed that there were two small holes in her back consistent with wounds caused by a small calibre firearm.

Don immediately had the post-mortem halted when it was confirmed they were dealing with something much more consequential than an accidental death. Fred Mason, the Whitchurch Township chief of police, happened to be a patient in the very same hospital. Hillock went to see him.

"I told him what we had and that I didn't think I could handle this, as we were a very small police force of fourteen that included only one investigator—me! I said that I thought we needed help and asked if he would authorize us to call in the OPP. He immediately authorized this and when Inspector Ray Williams of the OPP CIB [Criminal Investigation Branch] arrived later in the day, the post-mortem resumed."

It was quickly noted that Doreen had, in fact, been shot twice in the back and five times in the back of the head. Her hands had incurred defensive wounds, caused in an effort, no doubt, to protect herself. It was determined that any one of the head wounds could have caused death. For a brief time, it was unclear if there were seven, eight, or even nine shots, due to the extensive damage inflicted. However, there was never any doubt that there were more than six shots. The number of bullets were eventually determined to total seven, and the bullets were identified as "long rifle mushroom bullets."

Hillock soon deduced the weapon was most likely a less-popular 9-shot revolver, as opposed to the common 6-shot. This would explain the lack of cartridges at the site. In accordance with this theory, Detective Inspector Don MacNeil would later speculate: "Who shoots someone six times and then stops to reload and shoot a seventh?"

The once-idyllic home on the Bethesda Side Road was now a crime scene. It was scoured for evidence as a thorough investigation commenced to determine why anyone would take the life of this young wife and mother. Extensive air searches and full-scale ground searches were made around the property, but nothing of note was found. No suspicious persons or vehicles were noticed in the area, but the locals reacted swiftly to the idea that there may be a monster in their midst.

"The people in the area at that time were just out of it," said Hillock. "They were buying guns and the wives were getting their husbands to learn how to shoot. Everyone began locking their doors. It was unusual to even lock your door prior to those murders! In fact, during the door-to-door investigations, we would go to places where women would hail us from upstairs and I would say, 'That's okay. I understand, just let's talk.' People were terrified, totally terrified."

At times, Don would trail off in thought and his wife Joan would unhesitatingly take up the recounting of the events.

Hillock and Inspector Ray Williams soon joined Staff Inspector Archie Ferguson (who would later serve in the role of OPP commissioner) as a "war room" was established at the Downsview OPP Detachment. Ferguson took the lead in the Moorby case, and Williams would later head up the Helen Ferguson investigation. Hillock recalled the frenzy: "Soon, banks of phones were manned by officers and as the tips came in, we would follow up on all of them; boxes of Kleenex were on hand to take sputum samples from those we interviewed. This is what we did for weeks, seven days a week!

Both police and community were desperate to know how and why they had been visited by something so unspeakably evil.

—Don Hillock (seated at left) - York Region 1971.
(Courtesy of Joan Hillock)

CHAPTER TWO

The Ghost Knocks

"It is so much darker when a light goes out than it would have been if it had never shone."

— **John Steinbeck,** *The Winter of Our Discontent*

On the morning of Wednesday, May 6, Doreen Moorby busied herself with household chores. According to her friends and family, she tackled her daily tasks with punctuality: washing in the forenoon; the preparation of lunch around noon (which almost always consisted of soup and crackers); and at 1:00 p.m. she would put Brent down for his afternoon nap in his upstairs crib in the little dormer space of the A-frame. It was possible that on this day she was also preoccupied with upcoming Mother's Day plans, along with the anticipation of a call regarding some recently-completed tests related to her nursing career.

Doreen (née Sedore) was thirty-four years old and described as a "lovely person" by all who had come to know her. She was recognizable to many due to a youth spent helping her family run a small local grocery business.

At 9:30 a.m., an old family friend had arrived at the Moorby household in a 1966 Chrysler, ringing the bell inside the porch. Doreen responded moments later, having just finished bathing Brent in the bathroom. After she finished dressing him, she made instant coffee for herself and the visitor. They sat at the dining table that held the sewing machine and chatted. The visitor left soon after.

A second visitor, also expected on this morning, dropped by to discuss business that involved either carpet cleaning or installation services, presenting a miniature streetlight he had brought with him for the toddler. This visitor also departed after a brief visit, heading for Ajax and another appointment later that day.

Slightly later, at what was estimated to be after 10:00 a.m., a stranger pulled up to the tidy little house and emerged from his vehicle. He strode deliberately up the gravel path lined with tulips and daffodils, which faded in the shelter of a split rail fence. The stranger couldn't help but see the ride-on toys and other childish trappings discarded higgledy-piggledy amongst the unmistakable signs of a home occupied by a busy toddler. This was a house of light and laughter.

The stranger was clean cut, of medium height, with average features save for somewhat large ears, and most probably dressed in his favoured combination of checkered shirt, short jacket, and slacks. Many who knew the stranger would later reflect that he could blend into almost any environment, that he was simply unremarkable and often passed as almost invisible—"a ghost," some would say.

Doreen had no reason to feel any undue concern when the stranger knocked on the door—a door that was rarely locked. It is not known what the stranger said to gain entry. It would later be postulated that he may have asked to use the phone, or perhaps concocted a more elaborate ploy. Whatever was said, gain entry he did, and no doubt gained Doreen's immediate cooperation by brandishing a .22-calibre handgun. He possibly used Brent and the suggestion of harm to either him, her, or both of them in order to gain her submission.

What followed would inspire nightmares for both those who loved and barely knew her. Doreen was brutally raped in the bedroom and later—after being allowed to partially dress and pick up Brent, perhaps believing her nightmare may be coming to an end—stopped in her tracks by two bullets to the back, sending her to the floor and partially paralyzing her.

It was later determined that, as she attempted to crawl away with Brent still in her arms, the stranger fired five more shots into the back of Doreen's head. She held her hands up in an instinctive attempt to protect herself, and both index fingers were shot through. Brent was unharmed but pinned beneath her. The stranger could hardly have avoided the confused eyes of the little boy trapped beneath his mother as these additional shots were fired. Locking the front door behind him, the stranger was careful to leave as little evidence of himself as possible, even though the use of DNA was not yet in practice.

As the stranger—the monster—backed down the gravel driveway, mother and child remained behind, Doreen's lifeless body securing her son's body safely to her, even in death.

—Moorby Residence. (OPP Archives)

A thorough examination of the premises was conducted, revealing a truly horrific scene. "Corporal Charlie Rowsome of the OPP Identification Unit took fantastic notes and maintained great continuity of all exhibits," recalled OPP Detective Inspector Don MacNeil. The evidence was collected, identified, labelled, sealed in envelopes, and stored with the utmost care: when it was hauled out of storage thirty years later and the boxes dusted off, it remained perfectly intact. Rowsome's meticulous work was to prove absolutely crucial in eventually solving the horrendous murder.

During a search of the compact A-frame, it was noted that all the windows in the residence were closed and locked. The ground-floor bedroom's plaid curtains were open and the double-bed with matching tartan headboard was made, with no noticeable indentations in the pillows. The spread was slightly wrinkled, as though someone may have lain or sat across the bed. A long, mirrored dresser adjacent to the bed sported family photos, a white lace runner, and a jewellery box. A small teddy bear sat as if viewing the room guardedly through the mirror. A white bra and socks lay abandoned on the floor near the bed, and a pair of pantyhose lay across the end of it. A large quantity of blood had pooled in the bedroom doorway and soaked into an adjacent scatter rug.

In the kitchen, the stove drawer stood open, revealing pots and pans. In front of the stove sat an ironing board with an empty soup bowl on top, traces of soup and crackers inside. The pan holding the remainder of the soup sat on the stove, near the iron. On the counter sat an assortment of plates, mugs, and cutlery, as well as a box of crackers, a jar of instant coffee, and a kettle. A child's red pail sat in the sink.

Sifting through these photographs of the crime scene, I pictured a young mother with her son, familiar with how such a day may have rolled out: meals, naps, laundry, and play—but never this. It was incomprehensible, even disorienting. I kept wondering what the red pail had been used for.

It was a home that was dominated by a small and beloved child's presence. In the living room, bathed in natural light, toys lay scattered randomly before a stone fireplace brandishing a variety of trophies. A sewing machine was set up on the dining room table, with brightly printed material already being fed through the machine, the balance of it trailing onto the floor. The picture window, with curtains fully drawn, seemingly offered an eternal scene of rural calm and beauty.

On the bottom step of the stairs, leading up from the living room to the tiny dormer that served as Brent's bedroom, sat a freshly laundered baby blanket, neatly folded. It had probably already been taken from the clothesline at the rear of the house that still carried the remains of freshly-laundered baby blankets and clothing. Everything reflected a very normal sort of day— one that had been tragically interrupted.

ℵ

In order to develop a timeline for the day's events, the police spoke to both of the morning visitors who were known to Doreen. Both of their movements later that day were to be fully accounted for and eliminated them as possible suspects. Additionally, neither could recall seeing any clothes on the line during their visits.

It was obvious that some of the laundry had dried and been brought inside, like the neatly folded baby blanket on the bottom stair. Doreen and Brent had obviously consumed lunch, but the baby's crib held no signs of having been slept in. Slowly, a timeline was being established.

A call had been made to the house at precisely 1:50 p.m. that day to let Doreen know her final marks from the recent nursing exam, and the caller stated that she had allowed the phone to ring nine times before hanging up. It was a call that Doreen had been eagerly anticipating.

It was also discovered that a couple known to the Moorbys had driven west along Bethesda Side Road and past the Moorby home that day around 2:20 p.m. They stated that they had both observed a bed sheet on the line with one of the ends dangling free in the wind. They had joked that they would have to get after Doreen for being such a careless housekeeper.

Were Doreen and Brent's lives threatened to gain her compliance that day? Did Doreen know her killer? Had the stranger seen the attractive young woman previously, perhaps as she hung out her washing? Why had he been compelled to kill her after raping her? These questions and more would be asked by many in the days that followed.

ॐ

Doreen was found wearing only panties, slacks, house slippers, and an unbuttoned blouse. Her bra and a pair of socks lay crumpled on the floor beside her bed. Everything indicated that she had been allowed to undress herself and partially re-dress after she was raped.

It was believed that she was carrying the baby and fleeing from the bedroom when she was shot twice in the back, and it was determined at the autopsy that one of those shots severed her spinal cord. Doreen was thought to have crawled forward, clasping her hands to the back of her head before being shot five more times.

The pressure marks on the baby's legs would indicate that Brent had remained pinned for some time beneath his mother. A sole infant's slipper lay blood-soaked near her body.

—Brent's slipper. (OPP Archives)

Evidence also indicated that the killer stood directly over Doreen and Brent as he shot her in the head the additional five times. It was believed the killer then left by the front door, slipping the catch to lock it. All in all, they estimated the killer had been on site for just short of an hour.

A rape kit was completed and semen confirmed the donor was a type-A secretor, representative of about one-third of the population. However, in 1970, the science of DNA identification was still in its infancy. The following investigation included swabbing the mucous of as many male neighbours, associates, and friends in the Gormley area as possible, narrowing the base of suspects only slightly.

※

Don Hillock stood now in his kitchen, filled with the pungent smell of chili simmering on the stove. As though the aroma was stirring his memory, he recounted a lone detail which still remained vivid: at the rear of the Moorby kitchen, a full-length pantry door stood ajar, concealing the rear door of the house. He had always believed this might explain why the killer left so boldly through the front. "Odd how you remember things like that, but I couldn't help but think how brazen he was to leave that way!"

Not one single piece of physical evidence—such as identifiable footprints or fingerprints—was ever discovered, contrary to more than a few media reports at the time. Extensive door-to-door inquiries were made, and possible leads eliminated one-by-one.

For reasons not immediately apparent to most, more than one officer was to comment intuitively: "A cop did this."

The monster had made his debut on the Moraine.

CHAPTER THREE

The Ghost Knocks Again

"I know so many last words. But I will never know hers."
— **John Green**, *Looking for Alaska*

Mother's Day—on Sunday, May 10—came and went. In the meantime, the press made much of the ghastly murder on Bethesda Side Road. The small town and all of the surrounding hamlets were struck by rage and fear. A young mother had been raped, and then killed, as she protected her young son, spending her final moments not knowing if her son was to live or die. Many in the area were motivated enough to lock their doors, and more warily assess those who arrived unannounced, but all in all, it was still considered a random act. Things like this just didn't happen here.

The Humber River flows just west of Palgrave, another little gem of a town, sitting in the western boundaries of the Oak Ridges Moraine—the same moraine formed by ancient retreating glaciers that left huge deposits of sand and gravel behind. It was once a flag station for the Canadian National Railway and the small housing developments which sprung up in the early 1950s, soon to be followed by estate home developments and, subsequently, subdivisions by the late 1960s.

It was upon this similarly bucolic community that darkness and evil would also fall, and it would be many years before it was discovered that some of the daunting similarities surrounding the cases were purely coincidental.

Tuesday, May 19—just thirteen days after the Gormley

murder—would be recorded as a tremendously beautiful spring day. The Fergusons had moved from Ajax the previous September to the attractive, shingled, two-floor and four-bedroom stucco house. It sat on three acres of land off Highway 9 and just west of Highway 50. Russell Ferguson, a former botanist at Queen's University, said the family was excited about the idea of a country life.

—Helen Ferguson. (Ontario Archives)

The attractive thirty-seven-year-old Helen Margaret Ferguson was, like Doreen, a nurse who chose to stay home and raise her burgeoning family of three children, while her husband taught at Humber College. The couple was aware of the ghastly murder of another young nurse (who had also been married to a teacher) in close-by Gormley, but felt no undue concern for their own safety.

The family had already begun to make their mark on the little community. When all three of the children were in school,

Helen would often cross the open fields to visit and console a neighbour who had recently lost her daughter. "She was always offering to help in any way that she could," remembered the neighbour.

Early on that Tuesday morning, in consultation with her husband, Helen determined Dale, their eldest child at eight, was not recovering as well as expected from the mumps, and he should see their doctor again. Before Russell left for work, they decided Helen would call the doctor's office, and Russell would come home early enough to take Dale in to be looked at.

Dale was made comfortable in a downstairs bedroom where it would be easier for Helen to tend to him. This was a bonus for Dale—he would have the television to entertain him. His six-year-old brother, Scott, caught the bus for school as usual at 8:30 a.m., and the youngest child, Pam, aged four, only attending half-days, would catch the bus for school at 12:45 p.m. Helen normally walked Pam to the end of the driveway and waited with her for the bus, but on this day Helen was not feeling well and watched from the front window as Pam was picked up. The view of the road from the house was mostly unobstructed, as was the view of the house from the road.

The only visitor that morning was a neighbour who lived directly east of the Fergusons. The neighbour arrived at 11:15 a.m., chatted with Helen for about fifteen minutes and then left after giving her some lettuce plants. Both Dale and Pam were in the home during the visit.

It was approximately 1:20 p.m., about half an hour after Pam's departure, when there was a knock at the front door. Helen was ironing in the living room, while Dale rested in the downstairs bedroom, absorbed in *The Merv Griffin Show*. Dale later recalled that when his mother answered the door, the family dog had taken the opportunity to escape outside. Helen called after the pet and then headed outside to retrieve it.

A minute or so later, Helen re-entered the house by a door

that went directly into the garage. She likely used this door due to the fact that the front door had a faulty lock and could only be opened from the inside when it was closed. Because Helen entered this way, she needed to pass directly by the bedroom where Dale was, and he noticed his mother was being followed by an unknown man.

Helen explained to her son that the man had a sick boy in the car and wanted to get directions. Dale was apparently satisfied with this answer and went on watching television, believing the man and his mother to be nearby in the living room. Due to the television, he was unable to hear anything else until a loud crash followed by three loud cracks that sounded like firecrackers. In fact, he specifically remembered wondering why "that man" and his mother would be letting off firecrackers.

Shortly after, Dale saw the man race past the bedroom doorway to the door leading to the garage. This brought Dale to his feet, where he saw the stranger tear down a set of curtains, using one curtain to wipe the door handle, and presumably the other one on the outside doorknob.

Dale began to realize something was terribly wrong as the man quickly left the house and backed his car noisily down the gravel driveway. Dale called out for his mother but with no response. An eerie quiet fell upon the tidy little farmhouse.

Dale searched the house and found his mother in a pool of blood in the hallway, near the base of the stairs, her face a mask of terror. With uncommon presence of mind for one so young, Dale proceeded to immediately call the Orangeville Police Department, as their number was clearly posted near the telephone on the kitchen wall.

Dale spoke with Officer Fern Marchilda, who initially found it hard to believe the remarkable story being shared by the little boy at the other end of the phone. According to Marchilda, the young boy was so calm when he spoke that it was hard to conceive that his mother had just been murdered. Dale persevered and was eventually able to convince the officer it was true.

Marchilda called the Shelburne OPP Detachment, but the line was busy, so he called the Dufferin Area Hospital to have an ambulance dispatched as soon as possible. Shortly after hanging up, Dale received a call from the hospital requesting directions to the home. In retrospect, the boy handled the horrific aftermath with a maturity and calm demeanour far beyond his years. Dale then received another call, this one from the family physician, who was returning Helen's call in relation to Dale's slow recovery from the mumps.

Russell arrived home during this second call, at approximately 2:10 p.m. Neither the police nor the paramedics had yet arrived. Russell initially felt Helen might still be alive, hearing heartbeats as he pressed his ear close to her chest, but it sadly dawned upon him it was only his own heartbeat he could hear. Tragically, it was later estimated that Russell had arrived home only ten to fifteen minutes after Helen had been murdered.

Russell called the police and ambulance again to see why they appeared to be taking so long. This call was recorded at 2:20 p.m. The ambulance and Corporal N.H. Cummings of the Snelgrove OPP Detachment would arrive within the next twenty minutes.

As he and Dale waited outside on the front steps in the warm glow of a lovely May afternoon, Russell later recalled wondering to himself, "How could something like this happen on such a beautiful day?"

CHAPTER FOUR

The Mother Thief

"Do you remember running from our house? I do. It's clearer than my first kiss, the birth of my kids, or what I had for lunch today."

—Dale Ferguson, *Brampton Courthouse,* **August 7, 2001**

When attempting to reconstruct the sequence of events that day, it was presumed that upon encountering Helen, her assailant learned she was home alone with a sick child, and that he proceeded to tell her he was going to rape her, and to refuse or make a fuss would result in the death of both her and her son. The police also thought it was possible Helen made up the story about the sick boy in the car so Dale would not become unduly alarmed and get out of bed to see what was happening.

It was conjectured they next went upstairs to the bedroom at the west end of the house, to a room full of flowers and sunlight. The top sheet, blanket, and bedspread were thrown over the far side of the bed. Helen's blouse and slacks, both inside out, were found with her untied running shoes, bra, and panties, all in a heap on the floor near the head of the bed, which the police believed indicated that the assailant undressed her. One of the bed pillows was missing and found later to be on the living room couch, possibly indicating that Helen, reportedly not feeling well earlier that morning, had brought it downstairs earlier to rest her head on.

After being raped, Helen preceded the man downstairs, possibly believing the nightmare to be over. She was dressed only in her housecoat, which was not done up, and a pair of socks. All indications suggested that as Helen reached the bottom step, hopeful her ordeal had ended, the assailant shot her in the back of the head at close range, from only the second or third step immediately behind her.

He fired two more shots into Helen's back as he stood above her before fleeing the house. It was thought that a crash, which Dale reported hearing during the shots, may have been the sound of Helen falling against a divider loaded with glassware and sitting at the bottom of the stairs. Several scrapes on Helen's right leg were thought to be indicative of this theory.

While studying the police photos, I noticed the purported shelf/divider gave no indication of having served as a factor of Helen's injuries. In fact, nothing at all appeared out of place amongst the ornaments, vases, and bric-a-brac it held. Even though Helen's body had been removed before the police photos were taken, who would have replaced all the items symmetrically on the shelves?

—Ferguson Residence - Bottom of Stairs. (OPP Archives)

—Ferguson Residence - Chalk Outline. (OPP Archives)

Another puzzling factor within the same police photograph: the drawn outline of Helen's body and the blood-soaked carpet are well beyond the base of the stairs. Helen may have been moved by Russell from the confined space when he attempted to get a heartbeat. What can definitely be determined from the crime scene picture is that Helen's body was removed before the identification unit arrived. This alone would allow for potential confusion.

As in the Moorby case, no empty cartridges were found at the scene and all indications were that the weapon was a revolver. Dale did not report seeing the man carrying a weapon but believed his pants pockets were bulging. It was estimated Helen's murderer had been in the house for approximately twenty-five minutes, and most of the time was spent in the bedroom.

When the police looked for any indication of theft, Russell would suggest that as much as forty dollars may have been missing from Helen's purse in the bedroom. This, however, was never established as a certainty. Similar to the previous murder, no confirmed signs of theft were evident.

Something that did stand out in the crime scene photos were several vases of flowers—perhaps due to Mother's Day—reflecting the propensity for floral wallpaper throughout the home.

A post-mortem examination was made on the body of Helen Ferguson on the evening of Tuesday, May 19, at Dufferin Area Hospital in Orangeville, and conducted by Dr. G. M. Longfield of Brampton.

Helen had been shot three times. The first bullet had passed through the centre of the skull at an angle such that, if it had continued, it would have come out of the right eye; a second bullet entered her back, just below the base of her neck and to the right; and the third bullet entered just below the second. Helen's housecoat had two corresponding bullet holes with close-range powder residue at both bullet entry points.

Once again, Corporal Charlie Rowsome of the OPP painstakingly collected and preserved the evidence from the crime scene. As with the Moorby case, the murderer was identified to be an A-type secretor, and the bullets removed from Helen were identified as being .22 calibre. This information would lead to the assailant being dubbed "The .22-Calibre Killer" by the media and, in turn, the public. Furthermore, it was established that the same 9-shot handgun had been used in both cases.

The murderer had made more efficient use of his weapon this time, but the results were the same: a little boy was left without a mother, and this time with siblings to share the devastating loss.

Dale Ferguson was to describe the intruder to sketch artist Detective Sergeant Joseph Majury of Metro Toronto Homicide, who drew a composite of the suspect. Majury described Dale as "a remarkably astute and bright young man." Dale felt satisfied the composite sketch accurately identified his mother's killer. Photographs of the boy appeared in newspapers: a fair, tousle-headed, smiling child, seemingly without a care in the world.

Dale's description of the man was as follows:

Age: 38 to 42
Height: 5'8" or 5'9"
Build: Medium
Weight: About 160 lbs
Complexion: Dark, in need of a shave
Hair: Black, the style resembling a brush cut growing out
Speech: A deep voice, and may have had a slight accent
Clothing: Wearing what appeared to be a greyish blue sport shirt with yellow and white stripes and dark grey dress trousers

Dale added that "the man looked as if he had been in a lot of fights."

—**Sketch by Detective Sergeant Joseph Majury of Metro Toronto Homicide, based on description by Dale Ferguson.**
(**Ontario Archives**)

The local press saw an immediate relationship between the two murders on the moraine. This assumption was taken seriously by most of the locals, as doors remained securely locked and strangers continued to be viewed suspiciously. If someone unfamiliar was to knock at a door, they could expect to be answered only by someone at an upstairs window or from behind a bolted door. Everyone wondered "Would there be more?" and "Could they be expected to occur every couple of weeks?" Not to mention: "Was this Ontario's first serial killer?"

On May 21, Russell Ferguson and his three children, still in shock, sat soberly at the funeral of the young mother, grieving over the unreplaceable. Since Dale had identified the killer, and since Dale's likeness been identified through the media, Russell now feared his son's life was potentially at risk, and so all of the children were sent to the homes of other family members to be looked after.

As a huge investigation into the two murders got underway, and as the Ferguson family split apart, Russell wondered if "perhaps moving to the country had been a mistake."

A short distance away in Gormley, Albert Moorby struggled to deal with his own momentous loss and sought out the care of a doctor.

CHAPTER FIVE

The Boy from Cape Breton

*"It's not the size of the dog in the fight,
it's the size of the fight in the dog."*

— **Mark Twain**

I will always recall my first meeting with Detective Inspector Donald J. MacNeil. In an email, he had written to me: "I will be the old grey-haired fat guy that walks funny (arthritis). I will not have a rose between my teeth or a flower in my lapel but will be wearing an old OPP marine jacket with a Canadian flag over the left breast pocket."

I arrived early at our determined meeting spot, the delightful Mariposa Market in Orillia, and parked myself near one of the front picture windows so I could spot him entering.

I ended up waiting well past our arranged meeting time and couldn't see how I could have possibly missed his entering. I eventually decided to take a walk about the restaurant, and sure enough, there he was, alone in a booth, a steaming hot coffee before him, eyeing me warily. He had entered through the back door. I remain convinced he spent the entire time sizing me up.

As we engaged in initial pleasantries, Don took full account of everything going on around him, head slightly bowed and immobile, casting his eyes from side to side, and taking in all there was to see. I noted he could have described everyone and everything with exactitude if so required at a later date. I admit to initially feeling somewhat intimidated, but soon succumbed to Don's wonderful "Down East" sense of humour, which was sometimes irreverent and often self-deprecating.

Donald Joseph MacNeil was born in Sydney, Nova Scotia, in 1942. Like so many young people, he licked the salty taste of the sea from his lips and headed west to make a life for himself—this at eighteen years of age. Later in life, he would turn to the comfort of an unnamed rocking boat on an inland sea to find some peace and solace.

Don attended Sacred Heart in Sydney; his youth marked tragically by the loss of his mother at the age of fourteen. Don's older brother preceded him to Ontario, and Don was soon to find himself gainfully employed by the Toronto Dominion Bank for just over a year. He next tried his hand working for a stainless steel company out of Hamilton. For Don, these jobs amounted to stepping stones, as he aspired to embark upon a career with either the RCMP or the Royal Canadian Air Force.

One small detail proved to be a barrier for Don's future plans: he did not meet the height requirements of the day. As with Don Hillock, MacNeil would initially see his aspirations dashed due to what now seem oddly-restrictive physical requirements. But whatever MacNeil lacked in stature, he did not lack in tenacity. Don's son, Michael, later described his dad as being somewhat of a "tenacious little scrapper," and recalled hearing stories about his dad in fistfights back in the sixties and seventies. "It was a rougher, different era back then," said Michael.

One of the more amusing cases relating to stature requirements and policing took place in North Gwillimbury Township during the 1950s. Constable Carl Morton of Keswick not only filled the duties of police officer for the township, but also the roles of building inspector, truant officer, by-law enforcement officer, and dog catcher. Carl retired in 1950, likely by then worn to the bone. Needing a replacement, the reeve of the day determined they should hire a man who would literally fit into Carl's uniform—Carl had been wearing that same uniform since 1938.[1] It appeared that early hiring requirements were, again quite literally, the measure of a man.

The Ontario Provincial Police had its first civilian—Eric Silk, a career civil servant—serve as commissioner from 1963 to 1973. Silk was to sculpt a new identity for the force: along with the shortening of their moniker to OPP, Silk introduced squads and the parka, and had a brand-new insignia designed, one much like the badge sported today. Most notably for Don Mac-Neil, the height restrictions were relaxed. Fifteen hundred new officers were to be hired over a three-year period, and Donald J. MacNeil would be among the first five hundred.

On January 6, 1964, the "tenacious little scrapper" graduated as an OPP officer. Floyd Stewart—also a Maritimer, hailing from Prince Edward Island—was to graduate simultaneously. The two were to remain lifelong friends, oddly often brought together by chance.

The duo were soon affectionately dubbed the Gold Dust Twins. "I think it was E.W. Miller who, during our training, gave us the nicknames," Floyd suggested, speaking to me on the phone from Prince Edward Island, where he had retired. "We called him Eck Miller." With so many years having passed, it was hard to remember exactly what had inspired any of the nicknames, but that it was typical to have one during this era.

Initially, the young OPP officers were to spend two months at Toronto Division and then two months at Queen's Park. Headquarters was at 124 Lakeshore Boulevard: the first floor housed the Toronto Detachment; the second floor housed the province-wide detachment; and forensic sciences was housed in the back.

Don and Floyd shared a flat in Toronto's Bloor West area, residing on High Park Avenue along with four other young officers. According to Floyd, "It wasn't as bad as it sounded. There were lots of bedrooms and we all worked shifts."

In June of the same year, the Gold Dust Twins were transferred to Brechin, on the north-east shore of Lake Simcoe. "Our arrival brought the complement to seventeen and this would increase to a number in the twenties over the next three years," said Floyd. "It was expanding, but it was no fancy Lagoon City back then."

—Don MacNeil. (Kindly made available by OPP Museum)

They would generally work six days a week "on" in the summer months and five days "on" in the winter months. In 1967, with fate still determined to keep them together, they were both transferred to Grand Bend on the eastern shores of Lake Huron. That same year, they both married—Don in October and Floyd in November. They stayed relatively close geographically for many years to come, and they were never to lose touch.

Still today, every year on January 6 (the anniversary of their enlistment), the two connect, even if just by phone. With a couple of drams of scotch, they toast to "the good times, the bad times, and the Maritimes," which is "something Don made up," according to Floyd. It was one of many quotable lines I would hear "Don made up" over the years.

On July 5, 1970, Floyd was called to attend and secure the crash site of Air Canada Flight 621, which plummeted into a farmer's field while attempting to land en route from Montreal to Los Angeles via Toronto. All 109 passengers and crew were killed. Floyd recalled they set up a temporary morgue in a nearby arena in Woodbridge. "It was very hard emotionally, and I feel fortunate to have been able to compartmentalize that period of time in my life, avoiding post-traumatic feelings. I know that not everyone came away unscathed." Sadly, years later, Floyd would experience the momentous loss of his grandson, and I couldn't help but wonder if this proved much more difficult for him to overcome.

A little earlier in that same year, on May 26, Don MacNeil was also to become involved in a couple of notable cases. They would stay with him for the best part of his thirty-seven-year career. They would haunt him, but he would hang on to them like the "tenacious little scrapper" he was.

Don was a young officer stationed in Brechin at the time of the Moorby/Ferguson murders, and he was eventually called in to assist the task force being put into place, as it was anticipated these were only the beginning of a series of killings to come.

And so the boy from Cape Breton joined the esteemed group of officers who were to carry the case of the .22-Calibre Killer with them for the majority of their careers. He was also an addition to the increasing number who agreed there would be (and were) "more killings."

CHAPTER SIX

In Search of the .22-Calibre Killer

"The problem with putting two and two together is that sometimes you get four, and sometimes you get twenty-two."

—Dashiell Hammett, *The Thin Man*

The investigation of the Moorby/Ferguson murders was led by Inspector Archie Williams of the OPP Criminal Investigation Branch, and assisted by CIB Chief Inspector Ray Ferguson, as well as the Whitchurch Township Police.

A "war room" would be established shortly after the second of the homicides. Set up at the Downsview Provincial Branch, located at Highway 401 and Keele Street, officers were brought in from a number of districts to assist. Six extra phone lines were added to deal with the initial deluge of calls.

At the outset of the investigation, around four hundred police officers were involved in some aspect of the case. However, after a few weeks with no additional murders, the work fell to fifty officers, who continued to follow up on the still-considerable flow of tips. Nearly twenty thousand individuals were questioned over the first six months, and over twenty-two hundred tips had been pursued by June of 1970.

As early as May 20, it was established that the two murders were committed by the same person. The reasons for connecting them included not only the time of day the murders occurred, but the proximity of the homes, being only forty kilometres apart. Ultimately, the investigators were able to identify that the same weapon had been used in both the Moorby and Ferguson cases.

The *modus operandi* was also similar. Both women were taken into the bedroom, with their clothing likely removed by the assailant, and thrown to the floor at the head of the bed. Both women appeared to have been allowed to partially dress afterwards, and both were shot in the head and back as they were leaving, or had left, the bedroom. These facts confirmed—for me, at least—that the killer was a coward who could not bear to look into the eyes of the women he murdered.

—Moorby Residence. (OPP Archives)

The weapon in both cases was a .22-calibre revolver loaded with long-rifle mushroom bullets, with the suggestion that this was a somewhat-rare, 9-shot revolver, as opposed to a regular 6-shot.

The spermatozoa found in both women upon autopsy was from a type-A secretor; only 27 percent of the world's population falls into this category.

—Ferguson Residence. (OPP Archives)

The children in both homes had remained unharmed, and both women were attractive and comparable in height, weight, and body measurements. These details would always figure into my belief that both women had somehow been targeted and were not picked purely by chance. There were too many coincidences.

࿖

On May 22, the assistant commissioner of the OPP wrote to the deputy attorney general of Ontario: "As you are no doubt aware, these murders have been given considerable publicity. Concern is running high in the neighbourhood around the local area where these murders took place."

A reward notice, signed by OPP Commissioner Eric Silk, was posted by the Government of Ontario and the Townships of Albion, King, and Whitchurch, totalling $15,500 for information leading to the arrest and conviction of the person, or persons, responsible for the murders of Doreen Moorby and Helen Ferguson.

Officers were provided with the composite of the offender developed by sketch artist Joseph Majury (with the help of young Dale Ferguson). The sketch was distributed widely to the public in hopes of recognition.

The police were also armed with the information that the assailant may have been driving either a '62 blue or grey Rambler, or a '62 (or possibly '64) Valiant with primer paint on the right front fender. The police were to spend hundreds of hours over the next couple of years following up on what amounted to over three thousand tips and leads relating to the vehicle.

Five hundred and fifty saliva samples would be submitted to Dr. Frank Pinto at the Centre of Forensic Sciences, as well as cigarette butts from some promising leads in an attempt to narrow the search by looking for type-A secretors.

In July of 1970, Inspector Ray Williams was to state that "the murders have received wide coverage from the newspaper media, radio, and television. Public response has been overwhelming. The hundreds of pieces of information that have been received as a result are being evaluated and investigated."

During the investigation, roadblocks were set up in the general area of both crimes. Motorists were routinely stopped and asked if they travelled the route regularly. If yes, this was followed up with: "Were you in the area on May 19, and if so, did you see such and such a car?" If from outside of the area, visitors were asked if they were either salesmen or tourists, as in 1970 those were the two most obvious reasons for someone to be travelling any distance from where they resided.

—Wanted poster. (Ontario Archives)

Individuals who were known to have arrived or departed from Malton (now Pearson International) Airport during the crime period were thoroughly checked out on the premise that they might have travelled specifically to and from the area on a killing spree. All patients released from local psychiatric institutions within the year prior to the murders were also thoroughly vetted.

MacNeil spent time checking out construction sites during the investigation. "It was because of the transient nature of construction work," he explained.

There was no lack of promising leads. Some of the potential perpetrators happened to live in areas adjacent to the killings, some had a similar vehicle to the ones identified, and others exhibited behaviours that suggested their involvement.

After the Ferguson murder, a number of women came forward reporting that a man had recently come to their door but left very quickly when he realized there was another adult in the home. More than one of these witnesses referred to a Rambler as the car of the visitor.

At one point, a call came in to the Snelgrove Detachment from the homeowners of a property in Caledon Township that sat about twenty-one miles west of the Ferguson home. It was stated that a man matching the description in the police flyer had come to the home around 12:15 p.m. on the same day as the Ferguson murder. The man had asked the woman who answered the door the price of the property adjacent. She said that she did not know, but the man persisted, asking again "how much?" The woman repeated that she did not know, and indicated the real estate agent's sign, suggesting that the man call the real estate office for information, and ending the conversation. The homeowner described the car as a dirty grey '63 or '64 Valiant with red primer paint on the right front fender. She also stated that she felt instinctively afraid of the man.

Several more witnesses identified a stranger, often citing the sketch of the suspect, as well as noting the presence of a light-coloured '64 or '65 Rambler American. It would soon become an "accepted fact" amongst the public that the murderer drove a Rambler.

One potential suspect whose vehicle matched the description was seen crossing on the ferry from Tobermory on the Bruce Peninsula to South Baymouth on Manitoulin Island. It wasn't long before police officers ranging from Mindemoya to Gore Bay and Gogama to Manitowaning were conducting exhaustive searches. The driver and his vehicle were finally identified: The suspect was purportedly on his way from New Hampshire to Alaska to work and proved to be in no way similar to the composite sketch. (Incidentally, he was found to be in the possession of a .44-Magnum rifle and had a record for bigamy.)

Confident they could identify the weapon, "we looked for a 9-shot with everyone we interviewed," said Don Hillock. However, none were yet found.

Another early suspect was a recent transplant from Toronto to a horse farm near Gormley who had several charges of indecent assault against him, but he was soon eliminated. Also among those ruled out were a recently-deceased man and a newly-released convict.

Many others who were scrutinized had little more in common than being owners or previous owners of Ramblers. Thorough investigations were completed on suspects from as far afield as Buffalo, New York. "I worked on that case until I was raw!" recalled Hillock.

ॐ

Dr. Bruno Cormier of the McGill University Forensic Clinic gave an interview in May of 1970, offering up a brief profile: "The murderer has probably been living in the district for a considerable time and nobody suspects him capable of such violent crimes. He almost certainly has no police record. The mass murderer is sick, of course, but his psychopathology (mind sickness) is buried deep inside him. Periodically, it emerges, and when it does, there's a violent explosion. He kills, then acts normally again and goes about his business."

CHAPTER SEVEN

The Unusual Suspects

"The truth must be quite plain, if one could just clear away the litter."

—**Agatha Christie**, *A Caribbean Mystery*

In the course of researching this book, it soon became apparent that I would need to access as many sources of archived material as possible. If only for a short time, I let my imagination run free and saw myself wandering amidst the dusty basement tombs of a fantasized Ontario Archives, with some Canadian version of Indiana Jones eventually coming to my aid. Of course, this was not the case—and the reality of research did become a bit daunting.

After a period of both identifying the files I would need and what costs were involved, I connected with Aaron Foster, a freedom of information analyst and archivist who, in perhaps a less-sensational manner than originally anticipated, did turn out to be my proxy Doctor Jones.

Aaron explained to me that it was sometimes hard to unearth materials, as the archives are not the creators of records, but inherit them as they were kept by the creator, and so the records are often not organized very well. "Some records were digitized from paper format into microfilm, and consequently they would often destroy the originals, which was okay, except sometimes the digitization was poor and hard to read," he explained.

After what felt like a bit of a long (and fairly expensive) wait, I heard from Aaron. He had both good and bad news, but "more bad than good," sending my spirits dropping. The good was he "might have struck a goldmine, as there were nearly two microfilms worth of material relating to the cases." He had digitized the records from the microfilm into a PDF file, making them much easier to access. There were, however, thirty-three hundred separate pages. Aaron explained there would need to be a time extension of up to forty-five days on top of the seventeen that now remained. The rest of the bad news was, expectedly, additional fees.

After this virtual exploration of the digital tombs of the Ontario Archives finally concluded, I began the fascinating task of sifting through hundreds of pages of files.

ॐ

In June of 1970, a series of calls were made to a Catholic priest officiating at a church in Toronto, located on Jane Street, south of Wilson Avenue. The male caller confessed to the two rural murders and requested a meeting with the priest. The man was thought to have spoken with a slight Spanish or Italian accent and suggested that he meet with the priest at the Simpson's Warehouse on Lawrence Avenue. The priest complied, attending at the proposed time and place, but ended up waiting alone in vain for some time in the empty lot. He did, however, notice a car that slowly circled him at some distance, and he later described the car as a gold-coloured '66 or '67 Rambler.

Later that month, the mystery caller phoned the priest a second time, once again requesting a meeting. This time the priest suggested the caller meet him at the church at 7:30 a.m. on the following Monday. The caller agreed.

Monday came, and at about 7:10 a.m. that morning the priest peered out from the choir room and saw a man seated in the back pew of the church. The priest described him as male, white, between thirty-five and forty years of age, and approximately five foot eight or five foot nine, with a combed-back brush cut. He wore a dark grey jacket and a green checkered shirt with brown pants.

As soon as the priest approached the man, he fled from the rear of the church, with several other parishioners seeing him as he dashed away. No further contact occurred between the mystery man and the priest.

ॐ

Another notable incident which drew similarities with the Moorby/Ferguson murders occurred in October of 1970. A woman was waiting idly in a parked car on 5th Line in Innisfil, Ontario, while her husband fished nearby at a small pond, close to the currently-situated Georgian Downs.

A man suddenly emerged from nearby bushes and threatened the woman with a revolver, shouting at her to get out of the car. He was described as about five foot ten, in his mid-thirties, and wearing coveralls, a hat, and dark glasses, along with a strip of tape across the bridge of his nose.

When the woman refused to get out of the car, the assailant fired a shot towards the front left side of the vehicle before approaching and attempting to pull the woman from the car. Somehow, the woman managed to blast the car horn twice during the struggle, before being dragged towards the wooded area and struck on the side of the head with the gun. The man ripped off her clothes, demanding that "he needed them."

Alerted by the horn, the woman's husband arrived within minutes. As the assailant stuffed the woman's clothing into his coveralls, he now turned his gun on husband and wife, declaring, "all I need is your car," which he proceeded to commandeer, driving off in a northerly direction. The suspect closely resembled the likeness in the police sketch.

ॐ

Police were contacted by one frightened caller regarding a series of fresh grave sites that had appeared on a nearby property. The caller had personally witnessed a very suspicious-looking character attending the sites at all hours. However, it turned out the supposed graves were actually soil test holes dug by the Department of Health, and the "sinister character," no doubt a somewhat-offended employee.

A teenage girl (both a neighbour of, and former babysitter for, Helen Ferguson) reported a disarming incident that occurred on the day of Helen's murder. At about 4:30 p.m., a stranger had approached her family home to ask what was happening down the road, no doubt referring to the police activity at the Ferguson residence. The teen had said she didn't know and called her mother to the door as the stranger was making her feel very uncomfortable. Her mother stated she was also unaware of the reason for the police activity.

The stranger left, but returned about an hour later, telling the teenager and her mother a woman had been murdered. He then stated, enigmatically, "Isn't it funny? A woman murdered her baby in Caledon a couple of weeks ago!"

This stranger was later identified as similar in appearance and dress to the Innisfil attacker, as well as to the fleetingly-repentant man who had called the Catholic priest in Toronto. Had the police found their man?

ॐ

More than one cryptic letter landed on the desks of the investigating officers. One particularly strange letter, sent in

December of 1970, read as follows:

> *If you want the man who killed the school teacher in Palgrave, Ontario a year or so ago, you should talk to .... He is your man.*
>
> *You will find him in Caledon East. The gun is buried in the corn field near a large tree behind his house.*
>
> *I unknowingly helped him bury it.*
>
> *If he is convicted I will claim the reward by a duplicate set of numbers listed below*
>
> *123744899553450004444bbb*

Another letter, also dated December of 1970, was received after a television broadcast requesting tips from the public:

I wish to inform, in regards to a suspect showed on t.v. who murder two wifes north of Toronto. Haven't been found yet. I tell you what had happened. I seen a man at the bingo game in Welland some time last summer answering the description of a man, as I have a picture of a man cut out of the globe and mail. First night I saw him I report that to our provincial police here in St. Catharines. Out the next week I saw the man answering the same description I had. If you are interested to know the description and how he look like I would be just gladly give it to you.

Another particularly incriminating letter identified a married man with two children as the culprit. During questioning, this man advised the police the letter had most likely been penned by the husband of a woman he had had an affair with. The letter ultimately proved to be an act of revenge.

Officers diligently followed up on every tip, with some leads taking them right across Canada. One such lead took OPP

Superintendent N.A. (Nick) Perduk and Corporal Wayne Frechette, a newly minted polygrapher, to Kentville, Nova Scotia.

The suspect appeared to present an excellent match in many ways. He resembled the composite sketch to a remarkable degree, and at the time of the murders owned not one but two Ramblers, both similar to the one described in the circular. Additionally, the personnel records at the Brampton American Motors plant where the suspect was employed at the time of the murders indicated he had been off on sick leave on May 6 and had worked the evening shift on May 19. Amazingly, he was also a type-A secretor and had owned a 9-shot revolver. If all of this wasn't enough, he had been under psychiatric care both prior to and since the murders and was described as "psychotic" and "capable of violence" by his psychiatrist.

Sitting across from me, coffee in hand, with the tape recorder whirring softly, Wayne Frechette was to recall the episode vividly some thirty-five years later, as well as reflecting upon how the Moorby and Ferguson cases became front and centre more than once throughout his own long career.

"Nick Perduk and I flew to Halifax, Nova Scotia, and then drove to the mental health facility in Kentville where the suspect was housed. We had been alerted by one of the staff there, who, upon recently visiting the Brampton area, saw the remarkable similarities in the suspect to the man in the poster of the suspected killer. He had felt compelled to contact the OPP," explained Frechette.

"Upon arriving at the facility in Kentville, we were told that the suspect was in the cafeteria. We decided to see if we could pick him out ourselves with just the poster as a guide. We both did just that and it was immediate! Years later, I remember thinking that he was as close in resemblance to our sketch as was the composite sketch of "The Scarborough Rapist" to Paul Bernardo!"

Frechette and Perduk took the patient off-site after getting the okay from the facility administration. So, with the suspect in full agreement, they took him to a nearby motel where they set up for a polygraph test. "It was never really so much about the results of the polygraph, but more about the conversation that was generated," said Frechette. "After all, polygraphs were not admissible in the courts of law. The man appeared lucid and quite agreeable to the whole process, so we set up in a motel room, and Nick set up to listen from the next room. We spent four to five hours like this, breaking from time to time so that Nick and I could confer on where we would go from there. You can imagine our shock when the guy confessed! The elation didn't last too long though, as I asked him some qualifying questions like 'Where did you get a .38 automatic?' when, of course, we knew that not to be the weapon used in the murders. He responded to the questions and details affirmatively and showed a lot of remorse. Based on the information we already had, we were pretty much able to eliminate the Nova Scotia suspect. I still recall how both Nick and I agreed that the fellow was a dead ringer for the poster. We also thought that the picture of his mother that he showed us, and who he expressed to have huge issues with, showed a remarkable likeness to both of the victims! He talked about how his mother, caught up in the occupation in Europe during World War II, had put him in a Belgian orphanage for safekeeping. He went on to describe being 'abandoned for years' and 'sexually abused by both the staff and the other boys there.' Even his background seemed to fit!"

But not all of the drama had abated. During the very same afternoon, relatives of the suspect attended the Kentville facility as the officers were interrogating him offsite. The family were told by the administrative staff that their family member had been taken by the Ontario Provincial Police in relation to two murders in Ontario. The family, very alarmed, contacted the RCMP immediately to state the patient had been kidnapped. "The RCMP stormed the motel and we quickly had to assure them that the admin had okayed the whole venture, as had the patient, but it was pretty funny at the time," chuckled Frechette.

"We did follow up on the cars he had owned while in Ontario, at a later date, but nothing much came of it. It just all proved to be a very good possibility that was not fully eliminated for years."

꩜

Wayne Frechette grew up in Barrie, Ontario, the very city where he would eventually serve as police chief from 2000 to 2010. He described his young self as a bit of a "hellion," skipping school and drinking beer underage. "My mom often had to bail me out of predicaments during high school!" When Wayne's father heard his son was thinking of joining the OPP, he mentioned that he thought Wayne might be involved with the law one day, but he wasn't sure on which side!

In an interesting coincidence, there is a real-life connection between Frechette and myself: Wayne's parents and my parents-in-law were long-time friends. Both Ivy Burke (my husband's mother) and Jean Frechette (Wayne's mother) were war brides who came to Canada after World War II.

Ivy's husband Stan, my father-in-law, worked at the Brewers Retail store on Anne Street in Barrie for many years, and Wayne explained that if he was about to attempt to buy beer underage—twenty-one being the required age of the era—he would know "not to go to the Anne Street store where Mr. Burke worked. So, on this particular day, I got my dad's car and drove to what seemed like the ends of the earth: the Blake Street Brewers Outlet at the east end of the city, with my proof of age in hand. As soon as I walked in the door, who greets me but Mr. Burke! I blurted out something like 'Hi, Mr. Burke, just doing some errands for my mum and thought I would drop in and say hi!' What an idiot I was! I mean, how could I possibly know he would be covering at another store that day? How could I possibly present my proof of age that described me as one Archie Schwartz or something like that? 'Say Hello to your mum and dad,' said Mr. Burke, smiling after me. I remembered mumbling something and making a quick retreat. I was sweating bullets when I got back to the car. I think I avoided Mr. Burke for a time, but you know, he never, ever said a thing to my parents!"

Wayne's wicked sense of humour never seemed to leave him. "As a polygraph examiner/interrogator, I spent a lot of time in very small rooms with very bad people. No wonder I am a little twisted."

Frechette went on to describe how, years later, he would again be involved with the Moorby/Ferguson cases, both directly and indirectly. In the meantime, the OPP would be directing their attention towards another suspect, one who could not prove a more ideal candidate. He was most distinguished at the time as the "guy who drove around with a blood-stained baby's coffin in the backseat of his car."

CHAPTER EIGHT

The Red Herring

"There is nothing more deceptive than an obvious fact."
—**Arthur Conan Doyle**, *The Boscombe Valley Mystery*

One man, whether by intent or just plain happenchance, made himself an almost-perfect target for the attention of the investigating officers in the Moorby/Ferguson cases.

Donald Apostal was born in 1917 in Medicine Hat, Alberta, to Greek immigrant parents. As an infant, his family moved to Greece, remaining there for some sixteen years before returning once again to Canada. He later claimed he was not allowed to go back to Greece, and that his father had been executed by the Nazis. He purportedly went on to serve in the Canadian Merchant Marines during World War II. After the war, he became a mechanic and had a fairly brief marriage and a son from whom he remained estranged.

Apostal was to work at a Toronto-based company for many years, where he was described as a "terrific mechanic." However, towards the late 1960s, his work began to deteriorate drastically due to heavy drinking and adverse personality changes. His employer arranged for Apostal to get help with his addiction, but Apostal was to adamantly refuse the help, and so the company was forced to let him go.

He drifted for a time and was often given lodging by well-meaning acquaintances. But he eventually turned on all those who tried to support him, often threatening and abusing them. Metro Toronto Police would, at one point, remove numerous weapons—including rifles, a shotgun, and a revolver—from a residence where he was staying, in response to calls from the terrified homeowners.

He eventually landed work at a gas station in the small hamlet of Ringwood, which is now encompassed by the town of Stouffville. In August of 1969, the owner of the station, who had also emigrated from Greece, was kind enough to supply Don with lodgings at the rear of the gas station, as well as the use of a beige-coloured '62 Rambler.

Apostal was known by the gas station employees to carry a firearm in the Rambler, as well as a .22-calibre rifle in the garage—or at least until the owner asked him to remove it from the premises. He also, for no discernible reason, kept a baby's coffin on a shelf. He eventually took to carrying the small casket around in the back of the Rambler.

Those who worked with or befriended Apostal described him as a heavy drinker, a liar, and in possession of a violent temper. His female partner of twenty years was often seen with obvious signs of physical abuse. She eventually left him and took extra measures to conceal her whereabouts. Another former girlfriend expressed being "terrified of him." All of the women in his life expressed that he had a voracious sexual appetite, one that would likely today be described as a sexual addiction. He intimidated most women who knew him, even casually, threatening one with "you had better be careful or I'll rape you."

He adopted disturbing behaviours, like wearing Halloween masks at inappropriate times. He appeared to enjoy frightening people. At parties, after drinking, he would become maudlin and tearful, often taking to shooting a rifle into the night air.

One police officer recalled that he had been chased from Apostal's property with an unidentified weapon during a routine inquiry. Apostal had reported a number of break-ins at the time, but ultimately decided to take things into his own hands.

"He had set up a series of tripwires," the officer reported, "and had a shotgun set up to shoot the intruder." There was evidence of previous testing of the trap: a massive hole in the back door.

He exhibited his particular distaste for trespassers when he erected a rather lifelike gallows at the end of his property. A mannequin was hung from its feet, the head in a bucket, with a sign propped up below that read: "Keep out, anyone who enters here—this is you!" This seemingly juvenile gesture took on a much darker tone when it came from someone as menacing as Apostal, and surely gave hesitation to any would-be intruders.

Many described Apostal as crazy, but some suggested he was "crazy like a fox"—in other words, crazy when it suited his purposes. He told more than a few people "it was nothing to kill a man or a woman" and often boasted about taking lives. Everyone seemed to agree on one thing: he was a "crack-shot with firearms, even when he was drinking, which was most of the time!"

Donald Apostal was an enigma who cloaked himself in a mantle of exaggeration, aggression, and myth. Prior to the murders, he had experienced some brushings with the law, but nothing compared with what was to follow.

ℵ

On May 5, 1970, the owner of the gas station left for an extended visit to Greece. Apostal was to serve, in the owner's absence, as the signature licensed mechanic on site. The staff were to later relate that Apostal often left the premises over the lunch hour for anywhere from forty-five minutes to three-and-a-half hours. They confirmed this to be the case (to the best of their recollection) on both May 6, the day of Doreen's murder, and May 19, that of Helen Ferguson's. During these extended lunch hours, he was often known to visit the local legion.

Everything seemed to point to Apostal. The sketch that had

been developed with the assistance of young Dale Ferguson had enormous similarities. A car similar to his—a 1962 beige Rambler—was identified by one witness as seen leaving the Ferguson premises on the day of the murder. It was also duly noted that, like the priest's mystery caller, he had a European accent.

One of the earliest calls made to the police in relation to Apostal was from a small convenience store proprietor. The owner said a man, similar in appearance to Apostal, was often a customer at the same store where Helen Ferguson was known to attend. He was always very expressive in his fondness for the store-owner's son and would say he would buy him a horse one day. The proprietor noted that on the day of the murder, this man had stopped in to inquire about the "goings-on" with the presence of so many police down the road, asking what had occurred. Not yet aware of the murder, the owner responded he didn't know. The man returned shortly after to tell him it had been a murder, and Helen had been killed. This was all very reminiscent of the caller at the nearby babysitter's home. He too was similar in both appearance and demeanour to Apostal.

Police were to discover both Russell and Helen Ferguson had likely patronized the gas station where Apostal worked, supporting the belief that Apostal was at least aware of the Fergusons.

Two OPP officers from the Downsview Detachment, Constables B.C. Brown and A.J. Hatschinski—often assisted by G. E. Sallows of the Alliston Detachment—were to spend the best part of three years following up primarily on Apostal, reporting regularly to Inspector A.K. McLeod.

Some local residents were truly convinced of Apostal's involvement and began to arm themselves. Calls continued to come into the police regarding his unnerving habit of exhibiting a baby's coffin in the backseat of his car. Some of the callers suggested there was blood in the coffin and there was "a doll with the arms torn off" adjacent to it.

During the months immediately after the murders, Apostal would be admitted to Orangeville Hospital, where a physician was to describe him as having "a form of seizure where it was possible that he may commit certain criminal acts and have no recollection at all." Furthermore, during one of several hospital stays—often attributed to mental deterioration, due to his alcoholism—he was particularly abusive and threatening to one of the nurses in attendance. The nurse who reported the abusive behaviour identified him, once again, from the police artist's sketch.

The police began to carry not only the composite sketch, but also a photograph of Apostal to present to the ever-growing number of witnesses they would interview. Not always identifying the composite sketch, they would often identify the photograph of Apostal. The Innisfil victims who had been held at gunpoint more readily identified the photo of Apostal than the sketch, as did a witness who identified him as making a telephone call to a priest in Toronto to confess to the murders.

Police eventually obtained a warrant to examine his current premises. There they found a number of guns and ammunition, but not the weapon used in the murders of both Doreen and Helen. Apart from the firearms, they discovered a bayonet, knives, and a silver knife-like letter-opener. A lid from a child's casket was also discovered. Apostal simply dismissed it as an antique. Regardless, there was nothing incriminating that definitively tied Apostal to the two cases.

Calls continued to come in over the period between 1970 and 1973. A female postal worker (with a rural route that included Apostal's home) described being made to feel uneasy by the man, who would just sit in his car, near the mailbox, glowering at her. She refused to deliver his mail unless accompanied.

Police were informed that entire neighbourhoods were concerned about the presence of Apostal in their community, and some were not even sharing everything they knew due to the fear of retribution. Apostal continued to be regularly admitted to the hospital with psychiatric issues. He would express to all and any who would listen that the OPP "were out to get him."

The police eventually conducted a sputum test on their prime suspect, but due to the limitations in identifying even a probable perpetrator, it proved unhelpful. By 1973, Apostal's Rambler had been sent to a wrecker in Toronto. Police would scour what remained of the car, sending four winter tires and rims to forensics for soil testing. There were no viable results.

After an escalation of bizarre acts, Apostal was finally admitted to the Penetanguishene Mental Health Facility. Constables Brown and Hatschinski would move on to other duties by October of 1973. As the Moorby and Ferguson investigations appeared to reach stalemate, a hair sample was taken from Apostal and handed over to Charlie Rowsome, who placed it in an envelope before labelling and storing it carefully with the other evidence.

Finally, in July of 1986, with all leads dried up, the boxes containing all the evidence in the two murders were placed into storage. During the years to follow, the Ferguson family maintained their conviction that Apostal was a most convincing suspect and worked diligently to keep the focus of the police in his direction.

Their efforts were not forgotten. Years later, after the onset of DNA testing, when the Moorby/Ferguson cold cases were resurrected, the first act by then-Detective Inspector Don J. MacNeil would be to submit the DNA evidence from Donald Apostal.

CHAPTER NINE

A Life of Crime

"I constantly remind people that crime isn't solved by technology, it's solved by people."
—Patricia Cornwell

—Donald J. MacNeil. (Courtesy of Don MacNeil)

Crime units were first established within the Ontario Provincial Police in 1979. Each unit consisted of a detective sergeant, a corporal, and a district intelligence officer.

Crime Unit Number 9 served an area that spanned from Trenton to Gananoque and north to Bancroft, and the corporal working those areas in the early 1980s was none other than the boy from Cape Breton: Donald J. MacNeil.

As Unit 9 contained the bulk of the province's penitentiaries, Don spent a lot of his time inside one or another. This work would often coincide with his private life—holidays and wedding anniversaries were not exempt. In 1980, the Detective Sergeant of the unit called on Christmas Day, telling Don's wife, Shirley, that he had "good news and bad news." Don got on the phone and asked the sergeant for the good news first. "You're going to make some overtime!" When Don asked what the bad news was, he was told, "You're going to Millhaven!" Don reflected, "It became a bit of a joke that the inmates maintained a copy of all the dates that detailed my family celebrations!"

MacNeil's chosen profession involved much sacrifice. "I spent a lot of time on the road, often away Monday through Friday, and it wasn't unusual to be gone all week, then return home, only to be called out again! My wife pretty much raised our son Michael single-handedly. It became tiring, eating so much restaurant food. And I would often return home on a Friday evening to the suggestion that we order in pizza!"

In the process of conducting interviews, I spent numerous hours with Don, always showing up with blueberry muffins I'd made from my long-coveted Northern Ontario recipe. As with Don Hillock, I sat spellbound as MacNeil recounted the details of his life.

During Don's long and colourful career with the OPP, he was involved in a number of notable cases. One of the earliest involved a Metro officer in the horse division by the name of Merle Frederick Smith.

Smith and his wife, Agnes, lived outside of Longford Mills, about sixteen kilometres north-east of Orillia, on the eastern side of Lake Couchiching. At that time, a wealthy Italian contractor by the name of Joseph Chiavetti had a place off Highway 12, off the Orkney Beach Road and near Uptergrove. Chiavetti had hired Agnes, and their work relationship had grown into an affair.

Smith found out about the relationship. He discovered his wife at Chiavetti's cottage and confronted Chiavetti. When challenged, the contractor responded with something to the effect of "you can't afford her." Smith returned to his vehicle and pulled out a .22. As Smith aimed, Chiavetti proceeded to pull Agnes in front of himself, using her as a human shield. Smith shot three times and killed his wife instantly. Chiavetti darted to the house and attempted to hide in the shower stall, which is where Smith confronted him once more, shooting three shots to either side of Chiavetti, but only superficially wounding him. Dodging the cop again, Chiavetti managed to escape to his car, but Smith, with a clear view to the car on the driveway below him, shot twice through the windshield, and twice through the side window, killing Chiavetti.

Don arrived at the scene to see Smith cradling his wife's lifeless body and repeating, "I didn't mean to do it." Don confirmed the woman had no pulse and pulled Smith to his feet, telling him to "come with me."

Don recalled what followed. "He was an incredibly strong guy; I suppose from working with horses. I pulled out my caution card, which we still carried at that time, and Smith said, 'I've got one of them.' This was when I realized he was a cop. He pulled out his card and showed it to me. He was later charged with ten years for manslaughter, under provocation. I thought of the sentence as one year for every shot he fired."

Smith served his ten years in Kingston, remaining under protective custody as a former Metro police officer. He worked as an electrician on the inside. "I heard that a couple of inmates tried to take him on, but he took care of himself," added Don.

ℵ

Another of Don's more memorable cases involved a triple murder at a home in Adjala-Tosorontio Township, near Tottenham, during the mid-nineties. The dead were identified as: ten-year-old Ricardo Navarro; Ricardo's mother, forty-six-year-old Glennie Navarro; and Glennie's sister, Lyrister David, also in her forties.

There were no signs of forced entry at the home. Glennie and Ricardo had been strangled, and Lyrister had been bludgeoned with a hammer in her bed.

Neighbours told the police that the native Trinidadians had been living there for about four years. "We figured out that the son, Duane David, was living with an aunt in Richmond Hill while attending school," said Don.

The David family were proud of Duane and had helped put him through school. It was later determined the young man attempted suicide after the murders, but was not successful. He then fled.

After putting forth a bulletin on the missing vehicle, it was discovered in the United States. The trail then extended to Los Angeles, where Duane David had made a bank withdrawal. "I was glad to be going to Los Angeles," added Don, "as I had never been there before."

The investigators were dispatched to share resources with the LAPD, as well as with the U.S. Marshals. As Don explained, "U.S. Marshals are the only ones designated to seek out fugitives, according to the United States Constitution. We worked with the same team who was to soon be so publicly involved in the O.J. Simpson case—most notably, Mark Fuhrman. I had planned on taking the LAPD guys out for a beer, but the U.S. Marshals nabbed David before the LAPD!"

The U.S. Marshals took custody of David, so the Canadian investigators had to go through the U.S. public defender to be able to return to Canada with David. However, it so happened the public defender was quite fond of Canada—as a child, he and his father had been hunting in Northern Ontario and gotten lost. They had been rescued by the Kenora OPP, who had found them by air and dropped them supplies.

Suffice it to say, the public defender did not fight the extradition. "Don't worry, this guy is going back to Canada. We owe you big time!"

ॐ

Another case of note worked by MacNeil was the murder of Provincial Constable Tom Coffin. Coffin, aged thirty-two, was serving with the Southern Georgian Bay OPP Detachment. On April 24, 1996, Coffin was on duty when he observed a motorist whom he suspected to be under the influence of alcohol. This individual was Allan MacDonald, a captain with the North York Fire Department and a former chair of the local Penetanguishene Police Services Board, through which he and Coffin knew each other.

MacDonald was subsequently charged. He responded by threatening that he would kill Coffin for arresting and charging him. Regardless, MacDonald was found guilty of impaired driving and would soon thereafter lose his job with the fire department.

On May 31, 1997, during his off-duty hours, Coffin was attending the Commodore Hotel Sports Bar in Penetanguishene and watching a game on television with a friend. At about 12:30 a.m., MacDonald entered the bar, walked through the crowd, and—without saying a word—pulled out a gun and shot Constable Coffin in the back of the head, killing him instantly. MacDonald proceeded to leave the bar, returning to his home.

Don MacNeil was off-duty at the time: "It was a Friday evening and I would often join a group of teachers, firemen, and other cops at the legion in Orillia. I returned home that night and Larry Edgar, head of the CIB at the time, called. 'We've had a bit of a shooting at a bar in Penetang,' he said, 'and there may be a cop involved.'"

Don headed back out. "Everyone who was anybody, in and out of uniform, showed up as we attended. In fact, everyone but the police band was there! It was a media frenzy and the sheer numbers made it impossible to collect evidence until later that night."

MacDonald came along quietly upon arrest but received a few scuff marks on his face when taken down in the gravel outside. "I hate that," said Don. "Now we have to explain how he got them! They took him to Midland, where MacDonald and the police remained on camera from the minute they left the cruiser. I wanted 24-7 on this guy! I also wanted the Crown to know that it was a police-killing, and to have the best pathologist put on the case."

A bridge in Penetanguishene was later named in memory of Coffin—only a week prior to Don sharing this story with me. "MacDonald was charged with first degree murder," recalled Don, "and neither he nor I were at the bridge ceremony, I know that!"

Incidentally, Brian McGuire, the crown attorney on the Tom Coffin case, had also prosecuted the Duane David case, and would later make up part of the prosecution team against Ronald Glen West, or Ronald "Glenn" West as the media often mistakenly referred to him, adding an extra letter to his middle name.

ॐ

Don MacNeil was one of fewer than ten OPP officers ever to be seconded to a royal commission when, from 1989 to 1991, he served as an investigator on the Dryden Air Crash, a scheduled Air Ontario passenger flight that went down near Dryden, Ontario, on March 10, 1989, shortly after takeoff. Don was quick to acknowledge his varied career: "I have done a lot more than the average cop!"

One of Don's last assignments sent him to Cape Breton to investigate a cell death. He was with CIB at the time. The OPP's involvement was a request from the Cape Breton police, as at that time the RCMP policed most of Nova Scotia and were at loggerheads with the regional police. The region did not want the RCMP investigating, and so they called in the OPP.

"This guy in the cell had been arrested for drugs and when his sister saw him on the gurney, said that he had a lot of bruising," remembered Don. "The bruises were later determined to be the result of the arrest, but his actual death was caused by a drug overdose."

Don, in usual jokester fashion, told his superior he wasn't sure if he could go to Cape Breton, as there "may be outstanding warrants for my arrest!" Don and two other officers eventually set out "to find out who thumped him!"

The investigators ended up staying there for three months. Their final report included the recommendation that there always be an automatic inquest for such deaths in custody. This recommendation stands today for all cell deaths.

"It turned out that the guard who found the prisoner dead entered into the logbook—after the prisoner's death—that she had checked on him precisely every fifteen minutes on the dot, but as it turned out, the cameras indicated otherwise."

However, there was one case of Don's that eclipsed the rest. As his career drew closer to retirement, the opportunity arose to revive an old investigation that he had cut his teeth on: the Doreen Moorby and Helen Ferguson murders. By now they were cases as cold as the grave.

CHAPTER TEN

Long May You Run

*"Well, it was back in Blind River in 1962 when I last
saw you alive. But we missed that shift on the long decline ..."*

—Neil Young, "Long May You Run"

Neil Young's recollection of the little town of Blind River was
limited to the demise of his beloved 1948 Buick Roadmaster
hearse. Most travellers, as they motor east or west on the Trans-
Canada Highway, slowing or perhaps even stopping at this half-
way point between Sudbury and Sault Ste. Marie, remember it as
a pretty little spot hugging the shoreline of the North Channel
of Lake Huron.

The early French explorers made much use of the protective nature of the North Channel as a busy voyageur route. Fur
traders, loggers, miners, and others seeking natural resources
also utilized these waters. The North West Fur Trading Company, later purchased by the Hudson's Bay Company, built a fur
trading post there, leading many trappers to settle along the two
rivers that flow into Lake Huron: the Mississagi River and the
Blind River.

Originally called Penewobecong (smooth rock or sloping
rock), the eastern of the two rivers was renamed the Blind River
by the voyageurs, as the mouth of the river was almost invisible
from the canoe route. The settlement that grew at the mouth of
the river also adopted this name.

The eventual discovery of copper in the area sparked not

only the area's mining but also its logging industry: constructing the mines called for timber and planks. A sawmill built at the mouth of Blind River was once boasted as "the largest white pine sawmill east of the Rockies." The mill would close in 1969, due in part to a huge forest fire, and in part to difficult economic times. However, the mineral richness of the area once again sparked economic growth, as uranium was discovered and a uranium refinery was constructed just west of Blind River.

But in the 1990s, the town of Blind River became known for something else: the shocking and unsolved 1991 Rest Stop Murders, which were committed during the robbery of an elderly couple at a secluded roadside stop along the Mississagi River. The killings occurred just west of Blind River, at what the locals now refer to as "Murder Park."

And just as the Moorby/Ferguson murders became a preoccupation for Detective Inspector Don MacNeil, the Rest Stop Murders were to become a lifetime obsession for OPP Detective Sergeant Ed Pellarin, the area crime supervisor out of Blind River.

Ed Pellarin was the second youngest of five children born to Italian immigrant Luigi and his wife Eda (also of Italian heritage), who hailed from Kirkland Lake. Born and raised in Timmins, Ed attended Timmins High and Vocational School.

Luigi, being a very pragmatic man, insisted Ed back up his desire to become an OPP officer (just like his uncle, Ed Ziliotto) with a sensible trade, "just in case policing didn't work out." Ed, taking his father's advice, went to college for an automotive trade. "I'm so glad I took my Dad's advice," said Ed, finding the education very useful, regardless of his eventual vocation.

Reflecting on his teenage years in Timmins, Ed recalled that "it didn't hurt having Italian heritage and the benefits of early facial hair," when underage he desired access to the Maple Leaf Hotel on a Saturday night, not only to hear Stompin' Tom belt out *Bud the Spud*, but to maximize the enjoyment with beer.

—**Detective Sergeant Ed Pellarin. (Courtesy of Ed Pellarin)**

Pellarin joined the Ontario Provincial Police on November 30, 1987 and was assigned to the Blind River Detachment. A gentle bear of a man, Ed described his arrival: "It was quite a shock coming from the bustling city of Timmins to Blind River, where they roll up the sidewalks at 8 p.m." The town obviously grew on him, as he would later plan to retire there.

Ed met Charlene, a young nurse from Massey, at a local golf tournament, and they married in 1990. Charlene was fully aware of what she was getting into: "I knew that I had married a career cop early on—just the fact that he took study books on our honeymoon was my first clue! It wasn't easy being married to someone who was away a lot; sometimes six months under-cover turned into an eighteen-month ordeal when we had two toddlers and one on the way, but when Ed was home, he was very involved. I'm proud of Ed and his accomplishments, and think he has had a wonderful career with the OPP."

Ed and Charlene are the proud parents of three girls, all of them raised in Blind River. Kathryn describes her dad as a hometown hero: "Some superheroes wear a mask and cape; mine wears a uniform and a badge." Jenna knows that as a family they have had to sacrifice time with their dad, at no fault of his own. Emily explains, "my dad's work ethic has influenced me to become a very hard and meticulous worker," but her concerns for her father's safety haunt her to some extent.

Having spent half of his career working in detachments other than his own, time spent at home has always been a valuable commodity for Ed. He enjoys fishing and hunting small game. Being from the north, he treasures his bond with its rugged beauty, understanding this isn't a given for everyone. "It concerns me when I see guys posted from the south to northern, more isolated spots, and the culture shock some experience if they don't manage to assimilate." Ed's observations rang true for me, as I had cherished my years living in the north. While Ed was settling into Blind River, I was living a few hours east, in Lively, and content to stay forever.

Ed's goal was to become a criminal investigator, and he realized this ambition in 1991, earning a promotion to detective constable. In 2009, he graduated to detective sergeant.

Over the years, Ed has worked on several high-profile investigations, his work taking him across Canada and into the United States. Among his career highlights, Ed identifies the RCMP Pension Fund case, as well as working on the Sudbury Arson Task Force.

But there is one case that stands out—the case that altered Ed's career forever. It began in 1995 with a series of violent armed robberies, occurring mostly along the Sault Ste. Marie to Sudbury corridor, and apparently targeting women, the elderly, and the vulnerable.

CHAPTER ELEVEN

North Shore Robberies

"I have something else to tell you that will make the hair stand up on the back of your neck."
—**Ronald Glen West**

The 435-kilometre stretch along Highway 17 (more commonly known as the Trans-Canada Highway) from North Bay in the east to Sault Ste. Marie in the west launches those venturing north for the first time upon a historical and visually stunning journey. As descriptive (and sometimes puzzling) place names recede into the rearview mirror—names like Sturgeon Falls, Lively, Whitefish, Espanola, Spanish, Serpent River, and Iron Bridge—one gains a sense of history and discovery. Many a first-time traveller is compelled to investigate the heritage museums that dot the route.

On May 25, 1995, the third anniversary of his mother's death, the Ghost rode out. He enjoyed the open road and was somewhat of a compulsive driver, feeding off of the constant visual stimulation. He desperately needed money, and using questionable means to obtain it was not a new concept to him. Back in his teens, explaining away a number of grab-and-dash robberies, he had claimed to a friend that "if people didn't mind their stuff, they deserved to lose it."

The Ghost planned his crimes thoroughly. He never left a trail of receipts or credit slips. He could outsmart the law anytime he chose.

He launched a brilliant plan. Brian Langan, residing on

Queen Street in Sault Ste. Marie, was advertising a hospital bed for sale. The "Soo" was a reasonable distance from the Ghost's home in Blind River and wouldn't draw any immediate attention to him.

He headed out in his blue van. Prepared as always, the Ghost had a handy "travel kit," consisting not only of toiletries for an overnight trip, but, far more ominously, latex gloves, rope, a starter pistol, a replica pistol, and a wrench.

The Ghost met up with Brian and examined the advertised hospital bed. He promised to return the following day on the pretext of "consulting his wife" first. The next day, he surely did return. Brian invited the potential buyer into his home, and briefly turned his back to the guest.

Brian was to regain consciousness sometime later, having succumbed to a number of blows to the back of his head. He found himself gagged, an apron wrapped about his face, and his hands tied. Brian had been robbed of not only his wallet, keys, and $400, but also of any future sense of safety and trust. He was to later request that the Correctional Service of Canada keep him regularly updated on the whereabouts of his attacker.

Buoyed up by a relatively easy haul, the Ghost kept on trucking. On May 31, only five days later, he arranged to tour a rental property with the owner, Camillo Rovinelli of Sudbury. Secure from prying eyes, another older victim at his mercy, it was relatively easy to disable Camillo with three blows to the head from a steel wrench.

Although getting on in years, Rovinelli was to put up an admirable effort, kicking at the Ghost, who proceeded to pull a knife on the elderly man. "I need money, I need money, I need money!" he screamed at Camillo, who immediately offered up $450 from his pocket and urged his attacker to leave. Forced into the bedroom and told to lay on his stomach, blood streaming from the gashes to his head, Camillo expressed fear of bleeding to death. He was warned to do as he was told and assured, "you're a tough guy, you won't die."

Furthermore, added the Ghost, "I don't want to go back to prison." With this, he tied the old man's feet and hands, and pushed him into a closet. After hours of struggling, Camillo was able to pull several coat hangers from the closet rack above him, and with one in his teeth, and one hooked around the light bulb above, he was able to break the bulb, enabling him to cut through his bindings with the glass shards.

A week passed. It was now June 7, the anniversary of the Ghost's paternal grandmother's funeral, and a lack of funds had already again become an issue. He set out towards the western boundaries of his chosen hunting grounds.

Unhindered by daylight in his quest for cash and spoils, the Ghost entered the Holiday House Emporium in Sault Ste. Marie. He explained to the clerk, Mary Sarlo, that he was from Thunder Bay and in search of a gift for his wife. He was soon able to urge Mary to a concealed area of the store, and then produced a pistol, telling Mary he was about to rob her, and threatening non-compliance with her life. After tying her up and thrusting her into a closet space, he rifled through her purse, taking $480, several credit cards, and some costume jewellery. Two elderly men and now a woman had proven no problem for the Ghost.

Another week passed. On June 14, he rode out once again, kit in tow, back to Sault Ste. Marie, where he had already experienced some satisfying results.

Mary MacDonald of Valentino Furs and Jewellery was the next clerk to be victimized by the daylight robber. After threatening Mary with an imitation handgun, he managed to steal $30,000 worth of jewellery, watches, and other merchandise. Still unsatisfied, he then went through Mary's purse, donning yellow latex gloves in the process, Mary was later to report.

The Soo took notice. Police Chief Barry King warned the public to lock their doors.

Two more days passed. It was now June 16, the anniversary of his great-grandmother's death, the funeral of which he, as a teenager, had served as flower-bearer. The Ghost was still flush with a small fortune in jewellery and watches but had run out of cash.

He found himself in the area of Iron Bridge, where he called up a masonry worker about work he supposedly needed done. The mason was not home and his wife, Olive (Paula) Jones, relayed this to the caller. Half an hour later, the Ghost showed up at her house to speak again about the labour project. Paula kindly let him in "to escape the mosquitoes." The replica pistol was quickly produced, and a terrified Paula was gagged with a rolled-up t-shirt. The Ghost donned his trusty yellow latex gloves and pulled three sweaters over Paula's face before raiding the home. It was later discovered his haul amounted to fifteen dollars and two cans of pop.

Did this meagre bounty compound the Ghost's constant financial desperation, leading him to fundamentally compromise his attention to detail? Or was his impending misstep due to a narcissistic sense of infallibility, bolstered by the ease of recent crimes? Or—as some have theorized—did he actually harbour an unconscious desire to be caught? Regardless of the reason, he was about to commit a series of slips that would ultimately see him held accountable for much more than the robberies.

On June 20, the Ghost made his way to the Money Pit Pawn Brokers in Sudbury in order to pawn one of the rings he had stolen from Valentino Furs and Jewellery. He hoped to leave with hard cash in hand. Recklessly, he proceeded to use his own driver's license, which identified him as Ronald Glen West of 79 Woodward Avenue in Blind River. Additionally, he allowed himself to be captured by the store's camera.

There had been at least two armed robberies in Sault Ste. Marie and one in Iron Bridge when the Ghost came onto the radar of Detective Sergeant Ed Pellarin. The robberies were similar, involving either seniors or women as the victims. With the assistance of a forensic artist, a good sketch had been developed of a man in a hat and no other disguise.

Then, the breakthrough: On June 30, ten days after West visited the pawn shop, an officer from North Bay recovered numerous stolen diamonds and rings that had been pawned by West and could now be linked back to him by the driver's license. The ensuing joint investigation involved Blind River, Sudbury, and Sault Ste. Marie sharing files, photos, and copies of the jewellery that ultimately ended up in both Sudbury and North Bay. The sketch proved spot on.

—West home in Blind River where arrest was made.
(Photo by Matt Burke)

A plan was formed to put West under surveillance until a search warrant could be obtained. Aware that West had children, and not knowing if they were present, Ed and his partner, Detective Robert (Bob) Furchner, arranged to arrest West outside of his home if possible.

A covert team set up surveillance in the Blind River boathouse of the Menard family, two doors down from the West residence. As they settled in to wait for the right moment, Kathleen Menard arrived at the boathouse in the midst of their clandestine surveillance with trays of sandwiches and hot beverages for the officers. Her gesture was flawed, but indicative of northern hospitality. "We loved Mrs. Menard dearly, but were concerned that West would catch on pretty quickly to our presence," said one of the officers.

They eventually spotted West on his phone, standing knee-high in the water at the rear of his home, and they descended upon him. A search of the house at 79 Woodward, including West's light blue '89 Chevy van, produced almost all of the stolen jewellery, including items that he had given to his wife, Reina LaCroix. Some of the jewellery was damaged, as West had attempted to pry the gems from their mounts. In the van they found the starter pistol and the robbery kit.

Reina was shocked to the core, having been under the impression that West was a diamond miner in the Wawa area. After digesting the news, she asked Pellarin if he knew that West had once been a cop. This was only the beginning of a series of revelations about the former Metro Toronto Police officer.

West vehemently denied any involvement in the robberies until faced with undeniable evidence, and he finally pled guilty after being identified in a lineup.

Was this just the tip of the iceberg? Were there other crimes in West's past? During an interview with Pellarin, West hinted at more: "I have something else to tell you that will make the hair stand up on the back of your neck." At the time, Pellarin thought West was referring to other robberies, which Ed assumed there were, and recalled thinking West didn't seem like the kind of guy to confess of his own volition.

On October 3, the forty-eight-year-old Ronald Glen West appeared before The Honourable Justice William Lawrence Whalen of the Superior Court of Justice in Sault Ste. Marie, only a few blocks away from Valentino Furs and Jewellery.

Assistant Crown Attorney Kelly Weeks prosecuted West on numerous counts of robbery, possession of stolen property, assault, confinement, and possession of weapons. The following day, Justice Whalen found West guilty on all counts and sentenced him to eight years, with a lifetime prohibition of firearms, ammo, or explosives.

The sentence seemed surprisingly lenient to some, who suggested West could easily have been given fifteen to twenty years. This was at least partially due to the revelation that Ron had been previously incarcerated for armed robbery in British Columbia in the 1970s. The justice explained his judgment: "To his credit, he has been able to lead a productive life, free of crime for some considerable time. I accept that he has been a good and caring father, and that is to his credit." Justice Whalen did, however, reference the age and vulnerability of West's victims: "All the offences involved violence and all imposed terror. They were an outrage to the community."

ॐ

When I communicated with Justice Whalen over twenty years later, he expressed surprise at the future revelations with regards to West's history and wished me luck in my research of a "very interesting and sordid piece of legal history."

Before being discharged to Millhaven Penitentiary, West penned a letter from his cell to the bewildered Reina, suggesting how to handle financial and personal situations while he was incarcerated. Reina, never to trust West again, promptly turned over the letter to Detective Sergeant Ed Pellarin. The letter would gather dust at first, but in time it would become instrumental in the unmasking of a monster.

CHAPTER TWELVE

Parallels and Lives

*"There is an odd synchronicity in the way
parallel lives veer to touch."*

—Ann Rule

I felt a very personal and compelling call to document this story:
the shocking crimes, the interminable wait for justice spanning
nearly thirty years, and the actions of those who were to finally
reveal the identity of "the Ghost."

Why? I knew Ron West.

My earliest recollections of Ron are of a rather odd young
man who seemed particularly uncomfortable around women. I
remember someone who faltered with speech at times and kept
his eyes downcast when addressing women directly. He would
often, with eyes averted, affect a slight grin, but that was all.

My high school memories proved to be similar to those of
a number of classmates I contacted some fifty years later. None
of us had imagined that such evil existed among us. In our faded
Grade 12 school yearbook picture, West grins uncharacteristi-
cally from the back row. It is hard to reconcile this face with that
of the last face seen by two young women three years later.

BACK ROW L-R: Jack McClelland, Gordon Wauchope, Bruce Wilson, Larry Townsend, Reid Robinson, John Johnson, Reg Madill, Ron West, Grant Oliver, Barry Rutledge.

MIDDLE ROW: Wayne Jorgensen, Earl Hand, Neil Noble, Donna Orr, Carol Oliver, Diane Laverty, Vera Kidd, Terry Smith, Ken Plester, Dale Rutledge.

FRONT ROW: Chris Hand, Betty Marie Little, Ann Payne, Yvonne Newell, Gail Parsons, Ida Linton, Anne Ritchie, Cathy Shouldice, Wendy Morgan, Larry McDonald.

12 A2

—Centre Dufferin District High School Yearbook, 1965.
(Courtesy of Ann Burke)

My life's work has been divided largely between social services and journalism. During the 1980s, I found myself happily landed in Northern Ontario's Nickel Belt with two small children and a partner who travelled a lot. I was soon to declare my new home as the best place in the world to live—as well as raise a family—and was quickly inspired to secure my long-postponed Canadian citizenship at Sudbury's City Hall.

I worked for the *Walden Observer*, a Sudbury-area newspaper where I not only sold advertising and did the layout, but also covered local council meetings, conducted interviews, editorials, composed fishing and gardening columns—and loved every minute of it. I was by no means an expert in any of these fields, but seized the advantage of sourcing out those who were.

The highlights of my time at the *Observer* were covering

part of Rick Hansen's cross-Canada "Man in Motion" tour, and a memorable rickety elevator ride to the bowels of the Creighton Mine. During this period I was also working part-time for the *Sudbury Star*, covering everything from children's performers to local up-and-coming musicians.

I would have been surprised then to know Ronald Glen West was just settling into the relatively close town of Blind River.

ॐ

By the 1990s I was to return to the Dufferin County area of my teens. I still freelanced, but also took on the full-time job of coordinating a rural community centre. Here the direction of my life would take a decidedly different turn, and indirectly account for the genesis of this book.

—**Highlands Rural Learning Centre. (Photo by Ann Burke)**

The Highlands Rural Learning Centre was located in the little hamlet of Honeywood, sitting high atop the Niagara Escarpment in picturesque Mulmur.

It occupied an old, red brick schoolhouse. Our services were directed to a large number of relatively isolated seniors, along with the area's children, many of whom were latch-key kids whose parents commuted to larger centres during the day.

We received a small amount of funding from the Ontario government and so spent much of our time fundraising, bolstered by the support of a deeply-committed board of directors.

On one particularly sunny September day in 1992—as I worked in my tiny office and as my sole co-worker, Youth Worker Lois Metz, bustled about, planning crafts for the day's after-school group—I was alerted by a fellow who had been hired to paint the trim on the outside of the school. He had noticed a commotion at the house across the street. He believed he had seen a child, covered with blood, being pulled into the house by a large man.

From my office I was unable to see the front of the house, so I quickly descended the front stairs and ran out of the centre, letting Lois know that I was going to see if help was needed. I knew the occupants of the house were relatively new to the village, and that both young girls who lived there had recently enrolled in Lois's after-school program. Other than that, I knew nothing of the family.

As I approached the house, I noted large pools of blood on the front step, as well as fresh blood still running down the door. Nearly thirty years later, I still recall the acrid smell of the still-fresh blood as I approached. Believing this must have something to do with an injured child, I felt a sense of urgency. I pounded on the door, listening for any kind of response, but none came. I ran around the house yelling (I can't remember what exactly) before finally returning to the front door. I pounded again and the door flew open. A diminutive woman, who could easily have been mistaken for a child, stood before me, covered in blood, a housecoat across her shoulders. Behind her, at the top of the stairs, loomed the large, threatening outline of a man, a wild look about him. I immediately understood from the woman's demeanour and her pleading look that this man was a threat. My only thought was to get this woman and myself the hell out of there.

I grabbed the woman, both dragging and carrying her across the street. We locked the centre's front door, and Lois tore off in search of some tea-towels to stem the considerable flow of blood from the woman's breast and hands. I called the police, all the time watching the house across the street for any movement.

The victim, obviously in shock, was still able to tell us the wounds had been inflicted with a kitchen carving knife and that her partner, the man in the house, was in fact a former cop and might have guns. Alarmed that several local residents had assembled nearby—having become aware of the commotion—I threw open a window, and using profanity I would rarely use, told them to take cover, as the large man now making his way towards the family car might be armed with a gun.

He left in the car, speeding off in a westerly direction. I called the police again to let them know of the man's departure and the fact that both of the woman's daughters were in school; We feared he may be going there. The victim, although under huge duress, was able to tell us about her terrifying ordeal and the days of bizarre behaviour leading up to the knifing. The victim felt the man may have attempted to poison her, and had made threats of harm while expressing his belief that she was seeing other men. He had also been drinking very heavily leading up to the day of the attack. Both Lois and I were in awe of her strength as she told us these details.

Help soon arrived, but it would take a few days before they tracked down the ex-cop. After her wounds were treated, the victim and her girls were housed at a local women's shelter. A pre-trial and trial ensued, and I received my initial education about domestic abuse.

During the pre-trial, the defendant sat at a table with his lawyer. When the victim was on the stand, I noticed the would-be murderer was making stabbing gestures with his pen. I couldn't believe no one else seemed to notice and mentioned it to the police officer next to me. When we came back from recess, the defendant was secured, handcuffed, and in the prisoner's box. It was not the first time I remember thinking, "Is he mad, or just evil?" Years later, when I heard of his death in jail due to a brain tumour, I thought he may have actually been mad.

During jury selection, I thought I recognized one of the selected jurors. We never actually acknowledged one another. In one of many coincidences, I was to later learn we had both attended high school with Ron West.

The ex-cop was to receive ten years for attempted murder, but died long before his release date. The victim and her two children were to relocate in search of a better life. To this day I treasure a small embroidered tulip in a blue frame the victim made for me as a thank-you.

I have been asked how I felt that day, and I have to confess I felt like a robot. I went to a cold, rational place where I didn't let myself feel much. I calmly gave all my information to the attending police, and one officer suggested the reality would hit home later. It did, and like a hammer. To this day I cannot tolerate being anywhere near sharp knives.

Two years later, I received a Commissioner's Citation for Bravery from the Ontario Provincial Police and a Certificate of Commendation from the Governor General of Canada. After our funding for the Rural Learning Centre dried up, I embarked on a career working for the same women's shelter that had supported the victim and her girls. I held workshops for the female residents, extolling the benefits of journaling in the process of their recovery.

ॐ

During 1998, while working at the Women and Children's Shelter, I ran into an old school friend, who alerted me to the two charges of murder that had been laid against Ronald Glen West for crimes he had committed in 1970. My friend told me Ron had joined the Metro Toronto Police force after leaving school. In fact, it was during this period that he had committed the two grisly rapes and murders. Recalling my experiences in Honeywood, I thought about the strange parallels. Another homicidal cop—it seemed so unlikely.

In the interim years, my work became social-service oriented, beginning with work at the Women and Children's Shelter and going on to include work in victim services and as coordinator at the David Busby Street Centre in Barrie. During this time, as a member of the Alliance to End Homelessness, I met with then-Prime Minister Paul Martin in an effort to draw attention to the huge number of homeless in need of mental health support.

Upon retiring, and over fifteen years after hearing about Ron's murder conviction, I embarked upon the journey of writing about him. I hoped my earlier recognition from the OPP might open the door, if just a crack, for me to be able to contact some of the key players who solved one of the oldest cold cases in Canadian history at that time.

CHAPTER THIRTEEN

Monsters Walk Among Us

*"Let me state unequivocally that there is no such thing as the
person who at age thirty-five suddenly changes from being perfectly
normal and erupts into totally evil, disruptive, murderous behav-
ior. The behaviors that are precursors to murder have been present
and developing in the person's life for a long,
long time—since childhood."*

—Robert K. Ressler and Tom Shachtman, *Whoever Fights Monsters*

Sitting almost directly northwest of Orangeville in Dufferin
County is the township of Amaranth. The historically swampy
area makes up a goodly section of the Headwaters, a precious wa-
tershed nestled between Lake Huron, Lake Simcoe, Lake Erie,
and Lake Ontario, with the Grand River coursing through it.
Amaranth, like its fellow townships of Melancthon, Mulmur,
Garafraxa, and Mono, possesses a name more reminiscent of
dusty tomes in your grandmother's parlour than that of a central
Ontario township.

Amaranth was at one time not only rustic but rural, farmed
by descendants of immigrants largely hailing from Great Brit-
ain. The amaranth flower grows abundantly within the township's borders, recognizable by its branching spears of mauve
and purple shoots, and often seen in ditches and along the dusty
roads. It would seem most likely that it is for this weed the
township is named, as opposed to the "amaranth, the imaginary
unfading flower of the poets."

In the 1850s, the small settlements of Amaranth—with such old-world names as Waldemar, Laurel, and Whittington—bustled with busy hotels and taverns appealing to travellers heading north. Later on, these would be deserted as the flow of travellers diminished, and the county dried up like an abandoned well.

Dry up it did, in more than one way, as it became a stronghold of prohibition in Dufferin County. However, as future generations of local school children happily learned, the area did enjoy a short period of fame for the enormous mastodon skeleton uncovered in 1890, later believed to have somehow been spirited away to Chicago, Illinois.

In the 1860s, with the threat of war between Canada and the United States looming, Amaranth forged its own branch of militia: the Amaranth Forest Rangers and Rifle Company Number One, which would quickly commence rifle practice among its members. They dressed in formidable dark green serge uniforms that included tams topped with pom-poms, and each member of the infantry was armed with an Enfield rifle. They made an impressive lot, but Dufferin County officials disbanded them shortly thereafter.

Inhabited largely by what one local referred to as "poor farm boys" in the 1960s, Amaranth is, in modern times, known as a prime source of bottled spring water, wind farms, and mega-quarries.

ॐ

It was to Phyllis Brown and Glen West of 10th Line in Amaranth that a boy, Ronald Glen West, was born on March 7, 1947. He was their first child. Most friends and neighbours of the West family agreed not only were they a handsome couple, but quite well off and modern compared to most local farmers at that time. Several young friends of the adolescent Ron were to say they considered Ron's life idyllic when compared to their own.

Ron was said to look most like his mother, and to be very close to her at one time, whereas his brother Carl, born some five years later, resembled Glen. There were persistent rumours that Phyllis's actual mother, Alma Brown, was represented to her as her older sister, and that Phyllis was raised believing her actual grandparents to be her parents. If this was the case, her father's identity was never acknowledged.

Glen coached hockey, including Carl's team. Alex Bell, one of the young players on the team, described Glen as being "a great guy and well respected. He wasn't one of those loud types. He was quite humble. Phyllis would often sit quietly by, always supportive."

ৰ

When I first visited Alvin Walker, he was recovering from a condition he had been warned he may never recover from. He now reported happily that he was even attending the gym. As we talked, Alvin petted and idly fed treats to the family dog, constantly at his side.

Alvin described himself as an early friend of Ron's, recalling how they became acquainted when both attended the same tiny schoolhouse. Alvin's dad, Ross, was best friends with Glen. In fact, Phyllis and Glen stood up for Alvin's parents at their wedding. "I've got a picture somewhere," recalled Alvin. "They were a good-looking couple, the Wests." This was a comment expressed by many. "Ten to fifteen couples, including my parents and the Wests, would gather on alternate Fridays at each other's homes during the winter months to play euchre. We kids would all watch TV or play crokinole. We were all very close back then. A group of we boys would sometimes play football, which Ron really seemed to enjoy, but not so much his brother Carl."

Alvin also recalled there was a boy at school whom Ron would bully mercilessly. But what Alvin didn't know was there was also another victim: Carl, who received the brunt of his older brother's nightmarish abuse. That wouldn't be revealed until much, much later.

A number of Ron's childhood acquaintances mentioned a disturbing event from their childhood. A trio of hunters had driven up to the area to shoot rabbits. As they walked along, rifles cocked, proceeding in single file along a dry creek bed on property adjacent to the West farm, one of the hunters was said to have fatally shot the fellow ahead of him. Ron was among the children who gathered when the body was brought out to the main road by wagon. The children were all very shocked and withdrawn—but not Ron. "He was eerily fascinated with seeing the corpse," a woman recalled years later.

Glen appeared to be quite indulgent when it came to Ron, allowing his older son to borrow his newly-purchased '61 Meteor anytime the boy was so inclined, resulting in Ron becoming known for driving one of the few flashy cars in the area at the time. "Ron always had wheels," said Alvin, "but he was a terrible driver. I would be scared out of my head when he drove." Others would also attest to Ron's terrible driving.

"Ron didn't appear all that interested in girls and I don't recall him ever having a girlfriend," said Alvin. "In fact, he seemed very shy around girls, whereas I was very appreciative of them!" Alvin also remembered Ron being a pallbearer at his ninety-two-year-old paternal great-grandmother's funeral at the age of sixteen. He was said by many to have been very, very close to her.

"Ron and I chummed around quite a bit until I was about seventeen," continued Alvin. "I stopped responding to Ron's invitations to join him after he started stealing. First it was cigarettes from a gas bar in Dunedin, and then it grew to be all kinds of goodies, whatever and wherever he could get his hands on them at other places like the Wasaga Beach/Collingwood Drive-In. I asked him once why he was taking the stuff, and he told me that 'if they didn't keep an eye on their things, then they deserved to lose them.' I didn't want to be an accessory, and I knew my dad would be very angry, so that pretty much ended our hanging out together. Besides, I didn't go on to high school, but remained home to work on the farm."

Glen purportedly died from cirrhosis of the liver in 1968. He was said to have been a heavy drinker. Ron was a police cadet by this time and, surprisingly, did not attend his father's funeral. "It was less than a year before Ron and Carl's mum was dating a man regularly," said Alvin. The new man in Phyllis's life was only nine years older than Ron and moved onto the farm early in 1970, but not before a huge confrontation between Ron, Carl, and their mother.

ॐ

Another early friend of Ron's began an earnest friendship early in high school. According to Carl Alexander, there seemed nothing wrong with Ron at the time. "If anyone had asked me who I knew at school that would gain the kind of notoriety attributed to Ron, he would have been the absolutely last person I would have suggested," Carl A. told me as we flipped through old school yearbooks, pointing out pictures that seemingly reflected the innocence of the era.

"I never went to their farm, even though I lived only five lines away," continued Carl A. "I thought his family were very attractive and progressive. They seemed financially well off. My brother was friends with one of the Walkers, as well as the Prices—neighbours and friends of the Wests—and this was how we got to know each other. Ron was a year older than me, but I had skipped a grade, so we ended up in Grade 9 together at Centre Dufferin District High School in nearby Shelburne."

Carl A. recalled one summer in the early sixties when, "we would drive to Wasaga Beach on Sundays. Ron was a terrible driver but I never felt too afraid for some reason. I thought he was interested in girls, but I don't recall him dating or having a girlfriend. He was a pretty shy guy with a bit of a stutter." Carl Alexander's mother kept a diary where she expounded on much of the social goings-on in the area. Looking through it recently, he found several references to Ron: "Ron West was at Rock Hill Park, a local music venue; or Ron was at the Old Time Fiddle Contest, to name a few. He seemed to get around quite a bit." It was to Carl A. that Ron would express an interest in one day becoming a watch repairman and a jeweller. "I'm not sure why, and I wondered if he had a relative who was in the profession."

Ron failed Grade 12, and the two drifted apart. "I heard that Ron had entered the Metro Toronto Force, and later it was rumoured that he had banged up three cruisers, which did not surprise me, recalling his historically bad driving! I was also to hear that he had gone on to serve in the vice squad."

—West on the Metro Toronto Police Force.
(Courtesy of Don MacNeil)

That wouldn't be the last Carl Alexander heard of his old friend. "I was at a social evening in Brampton in 1974 when I asked a fellow, also named Ron, who I was told also served on the Metro Toronto Police Force, if he knew how my old friend Ron West was doing. He looked at me rather oddly," said Carl A. "Later that evening, the same fellow was to take me aside and tell me that he had had occasion to be taking a prisoner out to B.C., when, who did he run into but Ron—not working, but in custody!" The officer didn't approach Ron, who had left the force in '72, as revealing he was an ex-cop would certainly put Ron at risk behind bars.

"That was the last I heard of Ron for many years," recalled Carl A., "until the telecast in '98, when a suspect by the name of Ronald Glen West was said to be in custody for the murder of two nurses in 1970. I knew it was the correct Ron because of his middle name, Glen, after his father. It was the only time in my life that I ever bought the *Toronto Sun* as I knew they would cover it!" To this day, Carl Alexander has trouble accepting Ron committed the crimes attributed to him. "Perhaps he was ill and failed to take his meds. I don't believe he had the capability to carry out such terrible acts." I was to hear this conclusion from more than one of West's friends.

ॐ

Harry Price attended the same one-room schoolhouse as Ron West and Alvin Walker. Like Alvin, Harry left formal schooling after Grade 8 to help on the farm, but ultimately went on to become a successful businessman in the stainless-steel manufacturing business.

When asked about Ron and the murders, Harry expressed the same shock and denial as Carl Alexander. However, he did recall the shooting incident from their childhood, along with Ron's seemingly bizarre curiosity. Harry's wife, Norma, had also known the Wests, as she had lived nearby. Joanne Matkowski, a friend of Norma's, had married West's brother Carl, and Norma would share the shock of Carl's sudden disappearance after Ron's sentencing in the early 2000s. Norma said Joanne had asked the police at the time to find him, which they did, but then reported back to her that "Carl did not want to be found."

Another individual who came to know the Wests quite well was Joanne's brother, Larry Matkowski. I first met with Larry at a quiet coffee shop, incidentally not far from the Ferguson home where Helen had been murdered. I had caught Larry between shifts, as he was currently working two jobs. It was immediately apparent to me that he was deeply troubled by the West saga, but that his concerns revolved more around the fate of his former brother-in-law, Carl West.

Larry and his family moved to nearby Melancthon from Toronto when Larry was quite young. Larry was about eleven years younger than Ron, but he would become closely acquainted with Carl.

Larry eventually became a police officer, serving with the Dufferin Detachment of the Ontario Provincial Police. Looking back, Larry recalled that both Ron and Carl were very polite, and that Ron was particularly quiet. "Carl was physically bigger than Ron, even though he was younger," said Larry. Ron and Carl were to stay with Larry for several days, holed up at Larry's mother's apartment in Shelburne—she and her husband had separated—during the huge April storm of 1975, which stranded many. This would have been shortly after West had returned from his "stay" in British Columbia.

According to Larry, the entire West family seemed to have alcohol addiction issues. "Carl couldn't have been more different from my sister. She barely drank at all. They had met in high school and become sweethearts."

Like his brother, Carl West also exhibited dangerous behaviour. "I will always remember, as a youngster, careening along

Highway 89 with Carl at the wheel and a friend of his in the passenger seat. I was sitting in the back seat, never more terrified, as Carl, beer bottle in one hand and steering wheel in the other, sped along at 140 miles per hour," remembered Larry.

"Later, my sister and Carl separated for a time, but got back together. That is until all the news broke about Ron and the 1970 murders. Carl just up and left—disappeared completely! He never returned to see his kids graduate, marry, or have kids of their own. I was to wonder if somehow Carl was involved in the whole 'Ron business' that surfaced.

"I had always thought that Carl was a very smart guy, and over the years after he dropped off the map—later, after I became an OPP officer—I would see if I could track him down, see where he was, how he was, but it was as if he had vanished completely. I was speaking to an old friend of Carl's—in fact, the very same guy riding shotgun on that memorable car ride— it was a number of years after Carl had vanished, and the friend said he had come across Carl living rough on his farmland near Uxbridge," continued Larry. "My sister was to divorce Carl at some point without ever setting eyes on him again. I often wonder now if he is still even alive. So many lives have been affected so gravely by Ron." The frown returned to Larry's brow. "Keep in touch. Please let me know what you find out."

I heard more from others. A story about a young girl allegedly raped by West, and whose family chose to keep it quiet, potentially to protect her. Rumours of fire-setting and bullying. It was extremely difficult for me to equate that shy boy with averted eyes to a monster under construction.

CHAPTER FOURTEEN

Ghost Mode

"Sexual offenders are usually experiencing stress at the time of their attacks, and I said such would be the case with this offender. The stress might be relational, medical, financial, sexual or caused by substance abuse. The rapist had discovered that the assaults momentarily relieved the stress and restored to him, at least for a while, his personal sense of power and control."

—Roy Hazelwood, FBI Profiler, *Dark Dreams*

In 1966, after completing a second term of Grade 12 at Centre Dufferin District High School in Shelburne, West enrolled as a cadet with the Metro Toronto Police Force. He attended Toronto Police College on Greenfield Avenue in North York, as this was prior to the establishment of the police college in Aylmer. At that time, he was five foot ten, weighed 147 pounds, and had blue eyes and brown hair.

Several of West's high school classmates had enrolled in the force around the same time as Ron, one in particular being Gord Wauchope, the former mayor of Innisfil, Ontario, and someone I personally remember as the class clown. "I used to play hockey with Ron. He was a very different character, a real loner," said Gord. "Years later, just prior to Ron being arrested for the murders of the two nurses, Wayne Frechette, who was chief superintendent, CIB of the OPP at the time, called me wanting to know anything I could recall about the guy, but as I said, he went largely unnoticed."

One of the young officers who may have gotten to know

West better than most was Keith Rogers. His family had immigrated to Canada in 1946. His mother was a war bride and his Dad had served as a Canadian soldier overseas, spending time in a prison camp during World War II.

I first met Keith in a Newmarket coffee shop. He was a tall man with an enviable shock of grey hair that put even Buck Martinez to shame. With an easy smile, Keith would tell me he initially encountered West in the same platoon at 53 Division. Rogers had just come off an undercover detail attempting to infiltrate a gang, and commenced uniformed patrol in April of 1970, just a month before the murders. "I guess you could say that we kind of hit it off, but we really didn't socialize outside of work," recalled Keith. "In fact, I'm pretty sure that Ron didn't really socialize at all. He never mentioned a girlfriend or his family at all. Ron was living in a basement apartment on Painted Post Drive in Scarborough at that time."

Keith and Ron would attend the firing range simultaneously. "That's where Ron first suggested that we go up to his farm in Amaranth for firing practice. I went twice, once over the early months of 1970 and then again on July 8 of the same year. I will always remember the July date, as it proved crucial to the events leading up to West's eventual arrest. He had been driving a red blacktop 1967 Dodge Dart at the time. We were jerking around and taking pictures of each other as we fired at targets set up in the field. I never met anyone at the farmhouse at the time, nor do I recall West entering the home."

After giving my conversation with Keith some thought, I later asked him by phone if he thought the target practice held at the farm was perhaps a kind of intimidation for those he felt had disappointed him: Phyllis and her new partner. He didn't think so, but it was food for thought. "You see, I never had any suspicions about Ron. He was just one of the guys on the shift, and back then, there was only one officer per car, so we didn't get to do a lot of chatting or socializing on the job."

Keith thought West may have been on motorcycle duty for some of his time at Metro. Keith also recalled a particular instance where he responded to an "assist police officer" call to support West, "who was being given a hard time by a drunk at a restaurant. The proprietor of the restaurant called us in, sensing that West may be in need of backup."

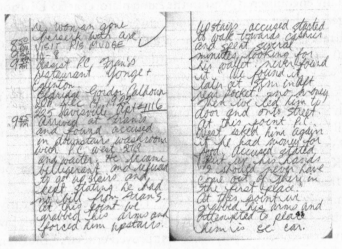

—Memo book entry. (Courtesy of Keith Rogers)

It would be nearly thirty years later when the cold case team, under the lead of Detective Inspector Don MacNeil, would use Keith's meticulous record-keeping to blow open the case against West.

In the interim, Keith would work on the hold-up squad, go to 54 Division and become a detective, take over the major crime unit, and then the drug squad. He also worked with the auto squad, investigating stolen vehicles and chop shops. "Sometimes we would come across a vehicle that may have a front end from Texas and a rear end from Sudbury. The stolen cars would often be shipped overseas in large containers, involving millions of dollars."

Keith also spent some of his career in charge of the Juvenile Task Force and had some involvement with Coventry House, identifying young girls brought to Toronto for purposes of prostitution.

ॐ

It was in early 1970 that dark clouds were building on West's horizon. A number of friends and acquaintances all clearly recalled a "huge bust-up" between Ron and his brother Carl with their mother Phyllis at the farmhouse in Amaranth in the spring of 1970. It was a little less than two years after their father's death; Ron had been absent since 1968, when he joined Metro Police. The reportedly heated confrontation was said to have been spurred by Phyllis' decision to bring a new man into her life. Her chosen partner was considerably younger: only nine years older than Ron. He promptly moved onto the family farm, and Ron was enraged. The murders were to occur within a matter of weeks.

Ronald Glen West—Metro Toronto Police, 54 Division, Badge 2719—would continue to serve, unremarkably, until September 5, 1972, when he left the force for what he described as "good employment opportunities." During 1972, he was known to sell the .22-calibre, 9-shot Astra-Cadix. He may have kept a Webley .38-calibre, 6-shot revolver, as well as other handguns and long guns that he had been known to possess.

West would now slip comfortably into "ghost mode" for a number of years hereafter, and only by sheer coincidence pop up on anyone's radar, when he was incarcerated for a series of armed robberies in British Columbia—the robberies his old chum Carl Alexander was to hear about.

The "good employment opportunities" included breaking into a series of medical centres in order to procure drugs. When confronted by a police officer in the course of one such opportunity, he would be arrested for robbery and for having concealed weapons: both a gun and a knife. West served his time and returned to Ontario. He was known to be in Shelburne in early April of 1975.

The OPP were later able to establish some timelines in relation to West's movements over the years. In July of 1967, West was known to have been in both Quebec and the USA. In October of 1970, he travelled throughout Ontario and again to the United States. In September of 1972, after leaving the Metro Toronto Police Force, he travelled through parts of the USA en route to British Columbia. Between 1972 and 1975, including the period of incarceration, he was known to be in Vancouver, New Westminster, and Burnaby in British Columbia. After his return to Ontario in 1975, he travelled again to America, this time to check in with a former fellow inmate. He also made trips to Newfoundland—ostensibly for mining work—in the fall of 1990. In early 1991, he travelled to the USA, visiting Tennessee, Michigan, and Chicago, Illinois. In the years leading up to 1995, he travelled extensively throughout Northern Ontario, including Timmins, Cochrane, Atikokan, Manitouwadge, Sudbury, and Blind River.

Many years later, Don Hillock, the first officer at the very first crime scene attributed to West, commented on these journeys. "He travelled out west, then south and across the States, eventually ending up in Blind River. Who is to say how many murders he committed?" Hillock was only one of a succession of police officers who shared this conviction.

West's movements between 1975 and 1988 remain somewhat blurred, particularly due to the secrecy and deception in his life. He spent a number of years in Pickle Lake, north of Thunder Bay, where he married Barbara Nayotchekeesic, a woman of Ojibwe heritage. Barbara and West were to have two sons during this period: Joseph and Gavin, born in 1982 and 1983 respectively.

West worked in a succession of mines during this period. Later, when the OPP were to attempt to record West's movements and actions, fellow miners, as well as other individuals with whom West had crossed paths, were unable to provide much information, as West had shunned friendship and avoided contact wherever possible. They simply referred to him as "a ghost."

CHAPTER FIFTEEN

Reina

"I am no longer afraid of monsters, because I once loved one."
—Emina Gaspar-Vrana

In 1988, Ron West, now a forty-one-year-old single parent, moved into an apartment in Blind River, Ontario with his two boys.

In the same apartment building on the coincidentally named West Street, sitting on the banks of the Mississagi River ("river with the wide mouth" in Ojibwe), close to where it merges with Blind River, lived Reina Lacroix. Reina had recently moved back to her hometown after a failed marriage in Montreal. Along with establishing a new life for herself, she had also come to assist her ailing mother. Still a reasonably young woman at forty-four, Reina suffered considerably from arthritis in her back, arms, and legs. She found employment working at a restaurant in the town and also found a market for her needlepoint.

At first, Reina tried to ignore the stranger who followed her on her evening walks and showed up in the shop where she worked. His behaviour seemed almost stalker-like, but she felt rather flattered by all this attention, dismissing his behaviour as simply odd. He seemed well-mannered, and Reina warmed to him.

She began to chat with Ron, as well as his two boys, outside the apartment building. Sometimes the two boys would set up a lookout for Reina from their apartment window as she returned home, and, shortly after they noted her arrival, West would be knocking on her door with a hot meal.

In 1990, Reina moved in with Ron and became a caregiver to Joe and Gavin, now aged eight and seven. The boys needed the attention—their apartment lacked even basic bedding—and Reina was happy to be doing something worthwhile. She described the boys as "wild and sweet" and anxious to please, not unlike many neglected children.

The boys were decidedly Indigenous in appearance, but West told Reina their mother was Portuguese, showing her a picture of a beautiful woman with a lily-white complexion. However, West informed Reina not to be fooled by appearances, as his ex-wife was a drunk and a drug addict and he had had to get the boys away from her. Shortly after, West was to head for Newfoundland, supposedly to work in an iron-ore mine. While gone, West proposed to Reina, calling on his cell directly from the mine, which he described as jutting out below the Atlantic.

The two were to elope in March of 1991, marrying at a chapel in Nashville, Tennessee. They had originally planned to get hitched in cowboy country in Wyoming but were thwarted by a blizzard. Reina had packed her divorce papers in case the chaplain asked to see them, and West claimed he had his in his suit pocket.

Reina was thrilled to have a second chance at love, and West seemingly treated her family well, throwing a surprise birthday party for Reina's mother, Marie LaCroix, as well as driving family members to hospital visits and appointments. It was Reina's older sister, Delina, who suspected something was very wrong. When she heard about the elopement, she had words for Reina: "You've just made the worst mistake of your life." A close friend of Reina's thought he was a creep and told her so. Additionally, Reina's aunt witnessed West dressing down his boys in public and felt his angry glare when she questioned him about it.

West still presented as a miner, but never seemed to be where he said he was; yet he never appeared to be without money. He claimed to own a diamond mine in Wawa and to be involved with a gold mine near Timmins. He would call Reina from these supposed locations during his absences but was careful to keep all telephone bills and bank statements under lock and key in the basement. This was also where he kept a rifle and a shotgun, both of which were to disappear shortly after two local slayings that occurred in a roadside park just outside of Blind River in 1991.

ත

The Riverside Tavern, once both a hotel and a restaurant, has stood on the banks of the Blind River since 1897. Currently, after being in the Kennedy family for sixty-seven years, it opens from 3 or 4 p.m. until about 7 p.m. each day, with either one of the Kennedy brothers tending the bar.

When I first visited the tavern, I was struck by the creaking wooden floors, which radiated a comforting smell of old draft spills and floor wax. The walls provided a visual record of the history of the old family watering hole. Brothers Kenny and Frank (Francis to those who have known him since childhood) continue to keep the tavern operative, even if for just a few hours each day; more a labour of love than income perhaps.

The frontage of the hotel on Woodward Avenue still clearly sports both a "Ladies and Gents Escorts" entrance as well as a "Gents" entrance. As Kenny Kennedy, bartender and long-time deputy mayor of Blind River tells it, "Before 1971, it was illegal to serve a woman on the gents side. To meet up with a lady, a gent would have to ask either of the bartenders to ask on their behalf for a lady's company, and the lady would have the option to say yes, the gent could come across, or she could choose to continue with the girls for a night out!"

The tavern is sometimes referred to as "The Museum Bar," and sports memorabilia is everywhere. Kenny is a huge Leafs fan and says, with the typical gusto of someone kicking a bad habit, that he has tried to give up on them and switch to another team, but only lasts about a day.

Kenny's brother Frank was a DJ at CKCY in Sault Ste. Marie back in the seventies. He clearly recalled Ron and Reina coming to the tavern for a couple of drinks. "I always thought I had a good eye for reading people, but not him," said Frank. "He would take Reina by the arm and guide her to the table, pulling his chair close to hers, and it would be Reina who did all the talking. He would remain completely attentive and she seemed ultimately to appreciate him in her life. I think that Reina was very vulnerable and rather naive, and tickled pink to be doted on."

Kenny saw West as a "quirky guy." Whenever he dropped into the tavern on his own for a couple of drafts, he would keep completely to himself and never chatted with the others at the bar. He sat alone and appeared riveted to the television screen. I could understand how that had seemed odd in respect to the group of miners who had just finished work on the day I visited: they stood three or four deep at the now-communal bar, and not one retired to the tables on either side.

Both brothers clearly recalled that Reina and Ron, along with the boys, later moved from the West Street apartments to a little house on Woodward Avenue, only a couple of houses down from the tavern itself. The brothers often saw them walking arm in arm along the road, totally absorbed in each other.

The house on Woodward, which had been owned by the father of Reina's ex-husband, sat close to the edge of Blind River, and featured a small boat house out back. This was where West was to be arrested for the robberies in 1995.

Another resident, Mel Hall—whose husband, OPP officer Andrew Hall, passed away in October of 2016 from Lou Gehrig's Disease—also had some recollections of Reina and Ron. Andrew had shared an apartment with Ed Pellarin as a young bachelor and fellow officer. Mel and Andrew were to later occupy a house only two doors down from West and Reina. This house had been previously occupied by Mel's mother, the same woman who had delivered sandwiches and hot drinks to the undercover detail in the boat house in true "Northern Ontario hospitality" fashion.

Mel recalled Reina as being "very tiny, and West appeared to tower over her. He was always very private, almost standoffish, quite a chameleon. I only engaged in a very brief conversation with him once at a yard sale that Reina seemed to have command of, and we only engaged in a few niceties." Mel continues to this day as a funeral director in Elliot Lake, at the same chapel where she has worked for over thirty-seven years.

𝒩

Reina liked how Ron doted on her, but not his drinking: he would consume a twenty-six-ounce bottle of liquor and a six-pack of beer most days. He also went out a lot after dark. He would be gone late into the night, claiming he went no further than the local Tim Hortons. However, no one ever noticed him there.

At one point, Reina was to ask West if the boys' mother wouldn't want to see them and asked if he had sole custody. West responded that Barbara was dead. This seemed counter to the claim of "divorce papers" in his pocket at the chapel in Nashville. Had West forgotten what he had originally told Reina about the boys' mother?

On road trips to Toronto and Chicago, Reina was surprised that a Northern Ontario miner, raised on a farm, would be so familiar with the downtown streets. Usually only cab drivers and police knew the cities so well. West also seemed obsessed with avoiding highways. Reina felt he seemed to keep a surveyor's map of the backroads of Northern Ontario inside his head.

At one point, West was to point out a lump on his head that he said his mother had given him, hitting him with a frying pan. It was proof of an abusive childhood, Ron had claimed.

The boys were not immune to abuse from their father, who would strike them, according to Reina, with little cause. After three years of marriage, West began to strike her too. The second time it happened, he proceeded to throw her out of the house and into the snow with only a nightgown on. "Your mother won't believe you," he taunted her, guessing she would go to her mother for shelter. "She'll believe me, I'm the good guy." Reina proceeded to speak to a lawyer about a divorce, but after a few days, in true domestic-abuser form, West sweet-talked her back home.

The boys became a handful. Joe, the eldest, tended to lead Gavin into trouble. Reina was frightened by Joe, who she described as having a "a man's anger inside a teenager's body." Reina insisted they see a doctor.

In the doctor's office, the physician produced a file that had been forwarded from Ottawa, where West had lived for a time. As West noticed it sitting on the desk between them, he came apart. West argued with the physician, who asked him, "You mean you haven't told them?" West replied that he couldn't, before claiming to feel faint and heading outside for air, where he passed out on the sidewalk. When Reina revived him, she asked what the doctor had been talking about. West replied that the boys' mother had died by suicide. He then sank to his knees. "How can I tell the boys she's dead? How can I tell them that she put a gun barrel in her mouth and blew her brains out?" West wept right there on the sidewalk, with huge tears falling down his cheeks. Reina softened once again.

Back at the house, West broke the news to the boys by telling them their mother had been in an accident: her car had plunged from a bridge and crashed into a river. Reina noticed how very good Ron was at lying.

One night, West stared at Reina while she watched television. She asked him what he was looking at and he told her, "I want to tell you something, but I can't because you're such an honest person."

By the spring of 1995, West's behaviour had become very erratic and the marriage was unravelling. Reina was fearful of Ron, who had become increasingly violent and possessive. He began to tell people that he had "cancer of the face" and then began to suddenly disappear, supposedly for chemotherapy in Sudbury. These trips later proved to coincide with the jewellery thefts.

Reina's tolerance of Ron reflected that of many women who wanted desperately to believe the angry outbursts and possessive nature of their partners was just a reflection of their intense love for them. It wasn't.

West also began talking to Reina about life insurance and what would become of the boys if anything happened to him. He mentioned there was money he had put away. She believed at the time that these actions were due to the cancer, and her strange and unhappy husband was dying.

Was West looking to move on? Once again, his lies were beginning to catch up with him. Would he pack up the boys and find a new start? Or was he resigned to being found out and taking what would come?

ॐ

The Ontario Provincial Police arrested West at the house on Woodward Avenue on June 30, 1995. He would begin an eight-year sentence for the north shore robberies and assaults.

Reina Lacroix's life fell apart. After the trial and West's incarceration at Joyceville Penitentiary, the boys were sent off to foster homes. Reina returned to an apartment in the very same building where she and West first met and lived.

Reina began to recognize there had been many clues to his double life. One particular instance remains intriguing to this very day. Over the years, West had spent a lot of time on his phone conversing with an unknown man, always out of earshot of Reina. She was to recall that this stranger, who called West regularly, only called one last time shortly after the arrest.

Sadly, Reina believed some of the townspeople held her accountable for West's actions, and thought she knew far more about West's activities than she ever let on. Rather the opposite would prove true: she was to play a large part in bringing West to justice for other, more horrible crimes, at which point she would be protected fiercely by the good people of Blind River from the media onslaught that would follow.

CHAPTER SIXTEEN

Chicken Bones and The Letter

"Talent hits a target no one else can hit;
genius hits a target no one else can see."

—Arthur Schopenhauer

In 1993, Don MacNeil was promoted to detective inspector of Criminal Investigations. He continued to juggle cases from Trenton to Thunder Bay, but when he heard an officer well-known to him had been designated to work on the Moorby and Ferguson cold cases, he excitedly asked for them, citing his history with the case and that he had a good suspect in mind. The officer suggested Don might be stretching it a bit, to which Don responded: "You don't shoot, you don't score."

The officer was happy to hand it over when Don received permission from the head of the unit at the time—the one and same Wayne Frechette who had travelled to Nova Scotia to interview and polygraph a person of interest for those very crimes.

Members of Helen Ferguson's family had worked doggedly to keep the investigation of the murders on the OPP's plate. Both the family and MacNeil were convinced that Don Apostal—long dead from brain cancer by now—was good for the crimes. Fortunately, the investigators were now armed with considerably more sophisticated tools, including DNA sampling.

MacNeil immediately got to work. "First, I had to connect with the Caledon Detachment, formerly Snelgrove in the seventies, as crimes stay within the district that they occurred in. Caledon would have maintained those earlier records."

Detective Constable John K. Smith of the Caledon Detachment was put in charge of pulling all the evidence together. "You know, Don was already past his retirement date, but he didn't want to retire. He was just plain persistent," explained Smith.

"The first thing we had to do in Caledon was look at Apostal as a suspect," remembered Don. So convinced was MacNeil that they had their man, he would later tell Smith, "We've got the guy, let's get a press release prepared!"

Not an hour after expressing his confidence, Don was to hear from the Forensic Centre's DNA specialist, Kim Johnston. Don breathlessly anticipated that his dreams had been realized. However, referring to the Apostal DNA samples that had been taken prior to his death, Kim was to offer most unwelcome news: "You're not even close!"

Max Haines of the *Toronto Sun* would later comment that this was the pivotal moment when Don "dug in." Max had assisted in keeping the crimes alive and in the public eye for the twenty-plus years he had run his true crime column in the *Sun*. His columns remained at the top of the Sunday *Sun*'s readership polls until his retirement from the paper on July 20, 2006. Not busy enough cranking out weekly columns, Max would also pen over thirty books.

Like MacNeil, Max hailed from Nova Scotia. His first book, *The Spitting Champion of the World*, documents the early years of the man who was to become Canada's best-known true crime writer. He describes his earliest jobs as bootlegger, chicken-plucker, naval cadet, and public speaker. Max got his literary start at a newspaper aptly called *The Casket* and would become as well-known for his delightful humour as his recounting of true crime—particularly Canadian crime. Don later recalled that when they finally nabbed the murderer, his first call was to Max.

With nothing else to go on at this point, Don continued

to check in with the various detachments within his seemingly endless boundaries. His diligence would prove invaluable. It was a visit with Detective Sergeant Ed Pellarin in 1997, at the detachment in Blind River, that would see Don's cold case begin to warm up. Ed was about to relate a very interesting occurrence to Don.

Ronald Glen West had been incarcerated since 1995 for the robberies. In the meantime, the home he had shared with Reina and the boys had been purchased shortly after his sentencing by a man named Garfield Roach. Roach had embarked on some extensive renovations and had recently discovered—secreted between the joists in the ceiling of the basement—a plastic bag containing pornographic photographs, several empty jewellery boxes, and not one, but two gun permits.

The permit that would be of most interest to Don had been issued for a Spanish-made, .22-calibre, 9-shot revolver, purchased by West on December 29, 1969. The permit indicated West was living on Painted Post Drive in Scarborough, and a Metro Toronto cop at the time. "I always thought that West had kept the gun permit as a souvenir," said Don, alluding to the habit of sexual sadists retaining a memento of their crimes.

Mel Hall was to say about the revelation that "all the stars must have been in alignment at that moment!

It was undoubtedly a eureka moment, as Don recalled Doreen Moorby's murder and the consensus of, "Who reloads after firing six shots to shoot once more?" It had been far more likely that the perpetrator had used a 9-shot pistol. Don also recalled that more than one cop involved in the early investigations had suggested "a cop did this!"

As Don started piecing his suspicions together, Ed Pellarin now began to wonder if there was a connection between West and the two roadside killings at a highway pull-off that had occurred within the Blind River area in 1991.

—The 9-shot revolver. (OPP Archives)

ॐ

The time had come for Don to pull a task force together. He assembled a group of six, including I.D. Officer Gary Savage, the designated "Keeper of the Evidence." Savage wasted no time in dusting off Charlie Rowsome's perfectly detailed and sealed evidence boxes, the materials pristine despite having been stored away for nearly thirty years.

Using the information from the gun permit, including the registration numbers, it was only a matter of time before the Task Force was able to track down the 9-shot pistol. The revolver was, in fact, quite unique. Made by Astra-Unceta y Cia, a Spanish weapons manufacturer, the model was not generally distributed within North America. Production of the revolver, based on the similar Smith and Wesson model, commenced in '57 and ended in '73.

—Examination of the revolver. (Courtesy of Keith Rogers)

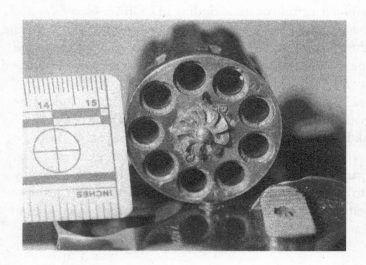

In another of so many coincidences, it turned out the revolver, sold by West to a pawn broker in Toronto, was now in the possession of an acquaintance of the task force, a person known to the family of Detective Constable John K. Smith.

Finn Nielsen, gun specialist and ballistics expert at the forensics centre, examined the pistol and felt that it was, in fact, the gun they were looking for. However, he was not prepared to confirm it based on the evidence before him.

The pornographic picture discovered along with the permits was submitted to the chief pathologist. MacNeil asked the pathologist if it was possible to tell if the woman in the picture was alive or dead. "Could be either," responded the pathologist. During the intense investigation that followed, it was eventually determined the woman in the picture was West's first wife Barbara, the mother of his two boys. It turned out she was still very much alive.

Barbara Nayotchekeesic had not seen or heard anything about her boys for many years when the task force contacted her. She related similar abuse suffered at West's hands as Reina, and confirmed West's addictions and behaviours during the time he worked in various northern mines. It became evident that Reina was not legitimately married to West, as there had never been a divorce from Barbara. West had been neither a widower nor divorced, and the fainting attack at the doctor's office had likely been a ruse to distract Reina from some sort of unpleasant information enclosed in his file.

MacNeil became obsessed with obtaining West's DNA. Now that they were aware of his bigamy, perhaps they could pick him up from the penitentiary where he was serving time for the robberies, and charge him. "I got this crazy idea that we could stop en route from the jail to the court for charges and offer to provide him with a chicken dinner. When he was finished, we could hang onto the bones and send them off for a try at a DNA match!"

When I later shared this scheme with Detective Sergeant Ed Pellarin, he raised his eyebrows. "I can't believe that Don told you that!" I was never sure if Ed responded with such surprise because the idea was just plain crazy, or because Don had actually revealed some secret police identification tactics.

However, another opportunity presented itself. During West's incarceration for the robberies and assaults, Reina had asked Ed if he wanted all of West's correspondence, along with the other packrat-like miscellany West had stored and locked up in the basement. She included a letter West had sent her after he was incarcerated, instructing her on how to deal with the finances during his term of imprisonment. Ed took the letter, along with the other items, and stored most of them in a filing cabinet at the detachment.

This led to another eureka moment—one that eliminated the need for MacNeil's elaborate chicken bone gambit. It may sometimes seem like self-adhesive stamps have always been around, but in the mid-1990s, one was still required to lick both a stamp and the envelope. West's letter to Reina was sent to the laboratory for testing. "We were getting pretty desperate by now, as indicated by the chicken bones plan, but the stamp would open the door to getting a blood warrant if it indicated West as a suspect," explained MacNeil. "The idea came to me after hearing about another case in Elliot Lake that involved threatening through the mail."

As they waited for the DNA results, the task force established that West had been at 53 Division on the Metro Toronto Force, and had shared a shift with Keith Rogers. They contacted Keith, and found he still possessed the duty notebooks which listed the days both he and West were off. Sure enough, both murders coincided with days West had not been working.

The notebooks also helped to identify where West spent time during those days off, identifying his proximity to the murder sites. In an era before the instant access of cell phones, officers were required to inform their detachment where they would be on their days off. It was noted that West sometimes vacationed in the Musselman Lake area, which was close to the Moorby residence in Gormley; and that when West visited his family's Amaranth farm, he would pass by the home of the Fergusons.

And as if all this information wasn't helpful enough, Keith had also kept a few photos that had been taken when he and West were "goofing around at target practice" at the farm in Amaranth. One of the pictures taken by Keith displays a confident West, kneeling beside the passenger door of his red-and-black '67 Dodge Dart, a cooler full of beer on hand, with the damning evidence of the 9-shot pistol clearly evident in the pocket of the car door.

—**West and damning evidence.** (Courtesy of Keith Rogers)

I will always feel that the binoculars also hold significance, in that he may have used them to stalk either or both of Doreen and Helen.

When the pictures were returned to Rogers, he would mistakenly rip them up, believing them to be copies. However, he realized his mistake and hung onto the fragments.

As the police continued their investigation, West's brother Carl was contacted and interviewed. He shared details of his childhood abuse at the hands of his older brother, relating that he had once been bound and threatened with being burnt alive. Carl had numbed a lot of this childhood trauma through alcohol abuse and had only just begun to turn his life around. John K. Smith was to reflect that "we re-traumatized him when all this came down." Carl also told the police that Phyllis, their mother, had been really hard on Ron in particular.

When the media laid out all the shocking details relating to the brutal murders, Carl would leave his wife and children, returning to the solace he found in the bottom of a bottle.

☼

After three interminably long months, Kim Johnston, the DNA analyst from forensics, finally got back to Don. "Are you sitting down?" she asked. "Because we have a match for the stamp!" The results indicated a 40 percent chance of West being their man—enough to seek a DNA warrant. Such a warrant allows the police to take blood from the suspect; even by force if necessary. "A blood warrant means that you can either put out your arm or we can punch you in the nose!" joked Don.

The judge in Brampton approved the blood warrant, but stipulated that they must notify West prior to the blood sample. Don questioned the logic behind this. "It isn't like we call ahead and say, 'Hey, we're on our way over to your house for 6 a.m. to take you by surprise and search your house for drugs!' Besides, the blood or West weren't going anywhere."

By this point it was January of 1999. The task force continued to pore through Charlie Rowsome's well-preserved evidence boxes, while West's lawyer in Blind River contacted his client at the Kingston Penitentiary in Collins Bay to inform him of the blood warrant.

On March 25, 1999, Officers Ed Pellarin and John K. Smith headed up the team that was detailed to take West's blood sample. I was surprised when Don told me that made a point of never dealing directly with West, but used his task force as the face of the investigation. "The only time we were face to face was in court," explained Don.

The whole procedure was recorded on video. West continued to insist that he was not the perpetrator, undoubtedly finding it impossible to believe evidence from 1970 would come back to haunt him nearly thirty years later.

Dr. Pam Newell of the forensics centre processed the blood sample. She quickly contacted MacNeil with the results: it was a match. In fact, a one-in-twelve-billion match. As Don quipped, "That would include everyone in the world, including the guys in the space shuttle!"

Newell commended MacNeil, saying that "Don stayed with the case all those years, and because of that, he is my star!" To this, Don responded: "That was a huge compliment, coming from her."

Don immediately called Max Haines. "We've got him, Max, we've got him!"

The media rush was instant. Carl Alexander purchased his first and only copy of the *Toronto Sun* to read all about it.

There would still be a trial for the families to suffer through, but they would now finally be able to put a face to the monster who had stalked their nightmares for nearly thirty years.

CHAPTER SEVENTEEN

Justice Served Cold

"The dead cannot cry out for justice. It is a duty of the living to do so for them."

—Lois McMaster Bujold

The preliminary hearing for *The Queen vs Ronald Glen West* took place at the newly erected A. Grenville and William Davis Courthouse in Brampton, Peel Region—the jurisdiction of the murders in 1970. The new courthouse served as the amalgamation of several smaller Peel Region courthouses, and also provided a home for the extensive library of the Peel Law Association. It boasted fifty courtrooms on floors one through four, and thirty-eight jail cells constructed within the basement.

West, currently serving time for the north shore robberies in Kingston, was now remanded to nearby Maplehurst Correctional Facility in Halton, where he would remain for the balance of the court proceedings.

Both OPP Detective Sergeant Ed Pellarin and Detective Constable John K. Smith would be responsible for transporting West to and from his appearances. They drove him back and forth from the jail to the concealed "sally port" (secured entryway) at the courthouse. "He was pretty talkative, but not about the case," said Ed. "I recall him being interested in the construction of Highway 407, obviously having missed a lot during his incarceration." The irony was apparent in the greater access that Highway 407 would have afforded West to both the Moorby and Ferguson residences.

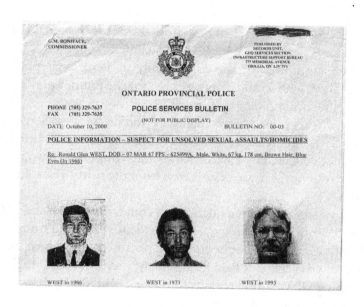

—**West as suspect in 2000.** (Courtesy of Keith Rogers)

"He would talk about his interests, like fishing, and life on the inside," continued Ed. "John and I felt we got to know him reasonably well. Whenever the actual case came up, he would say, 'you'll see that you've got the wrong guy.' Most of the time, John would drive and I would sit in the back with him. He was very clever and knew all the tricks of the trade, like the time he bounced up and down on the back seat of the cruiser and suggested we had a wire hidden. We would tell him that we didn't need a wire because we already had his DNA." Later conversations with the prisoner were to become far more intense.

The Honourable Justice Casey Hill presided and Assistant Crown Attorneys Brian McGuire and David Carruthers represented the Crown. West was defended by Kingston attorney D.G. Scully, along with one of Canada's most well-known criminal defence lawyers of the day: John Rosen. Rosen was most notable for defending Paul Bernardo, the notorious serial killer and rapist. Other clients of Rosen's included Dominic Musitano of the Hamilton Musitano crime family; and exchange student Min Chen, who would be prosecuted for the murder of nine-year-old Cecilia Zhang of Toronto.

The years peeled away when OPP forensics expert Sergeant Gary Savage presented the boxes of meticulously-maintained evidence collected by Charlie Rowsome. The evidence would speak volumes as it was resurrected from the thirty-year-old boxes.

The original DNA evidence had come from Reina and the stamp, leading Rosen to argue that evidence procured from "West's wife" could not be admitted because it was subject to spousal privilege. But Rosen's argument was unsuccessful. The damning DNA would remain admissible, and West's chances for acquittal dwindled almost to nil.

ॐ

Enjoying a sunny afternoon, a recently-retired Don MacNeil rocked gently to and fro on his newly-acquired boat, tied up at the dock in the Port of Orillia. Joining Don on that afternoon was Detective Staff Sergeant Scott James, who was still close with his old inspector. "Don was a truly great detective," remarked Scott.

James had joined the OPP in 1978 and had been with CIB since 1986. He had been serving in anti-rackets when he was seconded to Don's team and worked on the Ron West case for over a year. His duties had been largely logistic, keeping the team informed and up-to-date, cataloguing information, and connecting with the Crown. He also served as a conduit to West's lawyers.

A relaxing silence between the two friends was broken as

Scott's pager went off. It was Crown Attorney Brian McGuire. Scott called him back. "We were just prepping to hear the witnesses on Monday," reported McGuire, "when John Rosen called to say that West was copping a guilty plea!" The crown attorney could barely contain his relief. West's Kingston lawyer, Dan Scully, was to later tell the press that his client had decided to plead guilty in order to spare his victim's families the ordeal of a lengthy trial. No one I spoke to appeared to be convinced of West's motive.

Don Hillock, having recently testified at the preliminary hearing as to his actions at the Moorby crime scene, mentioned that he was surprised to receive a phone call telling him that he needed to attend again on August 7. "Did West plead guilty?" asked the astute Hillock. "I can't say at this time," came the response.

Hillock headed to the courthouse, ran into John Rosen in the court hallway, and asked him the same question. "He wouldn't tell me outright," said Hillock, "but he did say that you can't fight DNA evidence." Joan, at Don's side, confirmed this was what she had heard as well.

The morning of August 7, 2001 saw a packed courtroom. The prisoner was brought before the court, shackled and in handcuffs. The bearded and now-balding West, passive and emotionless, wore a rumpled grey dress shirt, black slacks, and a blue tie. For many in attendance, the shadowy figure who had haunted their nightmares for so long now stood before them.

It was a relatively small courtroom, housing seventy-five at the most. So many family members and friends of the victims were in attendance that the witnesses had to be seated in the jury box. Ed Pellarin, Don MacNeil, Scott James, and John K. Smith of the OPP were present, along with both Keith Rogers and Don Hillock, as well as Hillock's wife Joan, who had never previously attended court. Afterwards, all of them would vividly recall the powerful victim impact statements—a sober reminder of the families they had worked on behalf of, and the dead they now spoke for.

Members of both the Moorby and Ferguson families filled the morning with powerful and unforgettable statements. Tears flowed court-wide. The sheer horror of West's crimes and the impact they had upon the survivors was made real for all those in attendance—all, perhaps, except for Ron West.

Both Doreen Moorby's and Helen Ferguson's mothers spoke via videotape. They described how their lives had changed immeasurably since losing their daughters so tragically. Helen's mother, Jean, was almost ninety-two years old and had always hoped she would hear of an arrest before she died. For years, her son-in-law and grandchildren had lived in fear that the killer might return to eliminate any witnesses. Her daughter, Barbara Bell, and son-in-law, David Bell, had fought diligently for many years to keep the cases alive.

"How could anyone, in a senseless crime, take away a child's mother?" asked Albert Moorby.

Dale Ferguson was to deliver to a hushed courtroom one of the most powerful victim impact statements of all. "The last time I saw my mother, she was being carried away on a stretcher, covered by a sheet. I'll never forget her expression when I found her lying on the floor, her eyes half open, in a pool of blood. Beyond that, I don't remember her at all." Facing West directly, Dale challenged him: "Do you remember running from our house, Ron? I do. It's clearer than my first kiss, the birth of my kids or what I had for lunch today."

Ed Pellarin fought back tears as he glanced towards West to see what sort of impact Dale's words had on him. West looked directly back towards Ed, a slight smile on his face as he slowly shook his head, seemingly bemused.

I've wondered if it was the same yearbook smile from so many years ago.

Keith Rogers also stared right at West, but not once did his old target practice mate acknowledge him.

Don Hillock recalled his experience. "I was able to not only watch the victim's families from where I sat, but West too, and I have to say that there was no emotion from him whatsoever—there was nothing there. He was one arrogant son of a bitch. There wasn't a dry eye in the court and that included my wife. It was a courtroom full of tears." Joan Hillock would later relate that she was absolutely overwhelmed at the only courtroom attendance of her life.

Justice Casey Hill asked the prisoner if he had anything to say to the families. Remaining emotionless, he declined, showing no remorse before the court. "You are sentenced to prison for the remainder of your life," said Hill to West, who stood shackled at the front of the courtroom. Justice Hill also compelled the prisoner to provide additional DNA samples for the national data bank. These samples would be checked against cold cases, both existing and emerging, across North America.

"The public will remain seated," instructed Judge Hill. "Remove the prisoner."

ॐ

The sentence, however, was not exactly what it seemed. Being "sentenced to prison for the remainder of [his] life" did not necessarily mean West was being put away for good, as the life sentence was based on two (concurrently-served) second-degree murder charges. In 1970, when the murders occurred, Canada still supported capital punishment, and since capital punishment no longer remained as an option for sentencing, the charges were automatically dropped to second degree. This meant West, with time served for the 1995 robberies, could come up for parole as early as August of 2011.

As families, police, and the Crown exited the courthouse,

the media descended. Several family members vowed they would be watching the parole board and would attempt to block any future move to free West. "As long as I am here and have any strength left in me, I will sit in on every parole board hearing there is," said Barbara Bell, Helen's sister.

Ken Martindale, Helen's brother: "Two years ago [when the arrest of West was made], I thought closure had come. I'm glad it's over. I'm really happy. When he said 'Guilty,' I thought 'Amen.'"

Russell Ferguson, Helen's husband: "All I care about is that Ron West is out of circulation and can't do this again. I guess there is a certain amount of closure. I feel some relief today but the pain is still there. An awful lot was revealed to me by my kids today, hearing their victim impact statements. I trust this will have some healing for them as well." It was apparent that a number of family members had required psychiatric support over the years, and that some were still suffering from massive injuries to their mental well-being.

One other attendee at the court that day was Charles Foran, the celebrated Canadian author of such notable books as the multiple-award-winning *Mordecai: The Life & Times*. He was also Reina LaCroix's first cousin, and later penned an article for *Toronto Life*,[2] detailing Reina's time with West. Foran spoke to Don MacNeil, who he felt to be more responsible than anyone for seeing that justice was served. Foran also conversed with West's lawyer, Dan Scully, mentioning that he had written to West in Kingston, requesting an interview. Scully told him West had received many requests for interviews. Foran gave Scully his card and stated his connection to Reina LaCroix. "That probably won't endear you to him," said Scully.

Later that day, Foran would call Reina. She had been waiting for this moment for a long time, and Foran wanted it to be a moment of pure relief. "Now I won't have to be afraid any longer," she sobbed. Foran would wait until the next day to tell Reina that West would be serving the two sentences concurrently, and that he would be eligible for parole in a decade.

The general public still struggled to see how it could be purely coincidental that both victims had been nurses, married to teachers, and staying home with their children. "There was no evidence," said Crown Attorney Brian McGuire, "that West knew either of the victims, and likely we will never know why he chose them." McGuire went on to describe the crimes as, "incomprehensibly brutal and tragic in their result."

Ed Pellarin had attempted to unearth further insight into the inception of the murders, asking West in the back seat of the cruiser how he had chosen his victims. West was to confirm it was purely coincidental but refused to say if he used his police badge or gun to obtain the confidence of the victims. Ed also asked why West didn't limit his crime to rape—why did he kill both women?

West's response was chilling. "I don't leave witnesses. Everybody has to die sometime."

Pellerin felt that West enjoyed the notoriety, and that he was extremely arrogant. "Whenever we asked about any particular details, it was 'show me what you've got,' and then he'd make us work hard for a response."

John K. Smith agreed: "Yes, he liked to be in the limelight."

Both of them asked West why he had left the children alive, at which West became angry, responding with, "Who kills kids?" John K. pushed further, asking, "How could you leave those children to grow up without mothers and mentally scarred forever?" West chose not to comment further.

Years later, still struggling regularly with the workings of evil minds, Smith mused out loud that it would be comforting to believe Doreen's son Brent, only a toddler at the time of her death, was found pinned under her legs when discovered because West had placed him there to keep him from further danger.

I thought about John's comment for a long time. I concluded he may have been alone in suggesting any goodness existed within Ronald Glen West. Regardless, I felt warmed by John's faith in humanity.

CHAPTER EIGHTEEN

Murder Park

"Voices after Murder Park, in the damp, in the dark, maybe we should call the law ..."

—The Auteurs, "After Murder Park"

Sixty-two-year-old Gord McAllister and his fifty-nine-year-old wife Jackie, of Lindsay, Ontario, had embarked upon an adventure. It was a warm June afternoon in 1991, and they were on their way to Winnipeg, Manitoba, when they decided to look for somewhere to park their brand-new Winnebago motorhome and stop overnight.

It is easy to picture them enjoying a day of motoring at leisure along the North Channel route of Lake Huron, noticing the changes in the landscape as they travelled along the magnificent and ancient Cambrian Shield, grabbing fleeting glimpses of windswept white pine, with Lake Huron sparkling as in a Tom Thomson painting. They were barely twelve kilometres west of Blind River on the Trans-Canada Highway when they came upon a rest stop that skirted the picturesque Mississagi River.

It proved to be a beautiful treed space near the river embankment, a considerably private spot out of view from Highway 17—but clearly not designated for overnight stays. A government-issued sign confirmed as much: NO PARKING OR CAMPING 9:00 PM to 5:00 AM.

—"Murder Park." (Photos by Matt Burke)

But what would be the harm? There was nobody else around, and the picnic tables and facilities made it all too convenient for an overnight stop. Beneath the swaying fir trees bloomed the vividly orange devil's paintbrush, which at the time merely added to the wonderful ambience of what seemed to be turning into a delightful June evening.

The view was a bonus, and what a view it was: the Mississagi lay directly before them, dotted with silt islands that divided the loud and boisterous waters as they pressed their way to the bird's foot delta of Lake Huron. It was a slice of Northern Ontarian paradise, and they had it all to themselves.

The two enjoyed a quiet meal as the sun set upon this idyllic spot, and they ultimately turned their thoughts towards sleep and an early start the following day: Saturday, June 29. Life was good, and all was well with the world. There was not a hint of the horror and abject terror that would descend upon the elderly couple and a lone motorist that night; a night that would see the beautiful little rest stop henceforth dubbed "Murder Park" by the locals.

Jackie and Gord concluded their evening and drifted off to sleep, only to be awakened abruptly around 1 a.m. by someone pounding on the motorhome door. The visitor called out that he was a police officer and they could not stay there overnight. Upon opening the door, a man, armed with a shotgun, rifle, and flashlight, pushed his way into the motorhome, telling Jackie and Gord he was going to rob and then shoot them, but not until he'd had "a little fun" with Jackie. The couple were shocked, but obeyed the stranger's instructions, with Jackie offering up whatever valuables they had.

As she desperately dug through her handbag, the stranger, without a hint of warning, suddenly shot Jackie with the rifle. He then turned on Gord, who, though wounded in the back, was somehow able to bolt and get outside. "I rolled underneath the motorhome and I noticed that another car had driven into the rest area," recalled Gord. "And this guy had got out and was standing beside the car." The attacker turned his attention to the new arrival; Gord had been given a reprieve.

Gord's unwitting saviour was twenty-nine-year-old Brian Major of Elliot Lake. It was a most tragic case of being in the wrong place at the wrong time. Brian had pulled in to either use the facilities or simply eat his Burger King meal without distraction. However, he'd noticed that something was terribly amiss at the rest site and got out of his car. Quickly summing up the situation, he jumped back into the driver's seat, only to be shot through the windshield by a stranger, who was determined to leave no witnesses. Brian, a young husband and father, died instantly.

The gunman ran off on foot, with Gord still underneath the motorhome. "I was just lying there, just praying to God that he'd keep running, and he did. Soon as he went by, I rolled back out and got up and into our motorhome and drove out to the highway. I knew I had to get out onto the highway to get some help."

He eventually flagged down a trucker, but it was too late to get help for Jackie—Gord's beloved wife had already succumbed to her injuries. Of the three victims, only Gord, with minor injuries, survived.

Detective Ed Pellarin and his team wasted no time in investigating the murders. Extensive dredging of and diving into the Mississagi was performed by the OPP, ranging from the rest stop to as far east as Algoma Chrysler in Blind River, with the thought that the gunman may have ditched the weapons, or the valuables.

Detective Inspector Don MacNeil, reviewing the evidence, would never forget one particular detail: the Burger King wrappers amidst the blood on the front seat of Brian's car. Decades later, he still couldn't shake that image.

The lives of the families and friends of the victims would

be scarred forever. A long procession of cops in the years that followed wanted desperately to give some sense of closure to the survivors. As one of the officers involved in the investigation put it, "we need to speak for the dead." Another explained that seeing the impact upon victims and their families served as a huge motivator in his work as a police officer.

A witness came forward almost immediately. She stated that at a few minutes after 1 a.m. on the morning of the 29, a light blue van had emerged rapidly from the rest stop, careening towards and almost side-swiping her, before continuing east towards Blind River. The witness was unable to get a license plate number—understandably so, given the darkness and the suddenness of the event.

Police diligently checked more than thirty-five hundred blue vans on both sides of the Canada-U.S. border, but found no matches. "The fortunate situation here is that we do have a survivor," stated police. "Gord McAllister survived his wounds, and hopefully, he can point out the killer one day."

Gord described him to police as about thirty years of age, five feet ten inches tall, with a slight build, stringy blonde hair, and a receding hairline. Gord also assisted a forensic artist with a sketch, which was rapidly taken up by media far and wide. The police also turned to computer technology, hoping to possibly improve on the sketch.

"I'll never forget the look on his face," recalled Gord. "It wasn't a robbery gone bad. There was no resistance to this guy. He just simply was going to kill somebody for no reason."

Gord was later shown a layout of photos, among them the police's favoured suspect at the time. He didn't immediately identify anyone, but hesitantly gave it a second thought and then indicated the suspect, commenting that "number four looks like him"—but unfortunately this wasn't enough.

Reina LaCroix and Ron West were driving past the murder site a month or two later when she remarked to Ron that she hoped "the cops nailed the bastard who did this." West's response was icy. "The guy who did that knew what he was doing. They'll never catch him."

For two summers after West's arrest for the robberies, police divers combed the riverbed near Reina's apartment. It was rumoured they were searching for a blonde wig and a murder weapon. On seeing the sketch, Reina suggested the drawing looked a lot like West, but with a wig on.

☙

Gord McAllister eventually remarried, knowing some happiness again before passing away on Valentine's Day 2012 at the age of eighty-four. He would never know the identity of the monster who tore his life apart.

Brian's family continues to wonder if they will ever find some sort of closure in knowing who tore a husband, son, and father from them. Brian would be remembered as "an avid outdoorsman and a guy who would give you the shirt off his back." Iona Major, Brian's mother, praised the OPP for all their hard work, hoping one day Brian's murder would be solved. "I just hope they continue working."

Over twenty-four years hence and the beautiful little stopover is still known as Murder Park. The locals of Blind River will tell you that the night of June 28, 1991 was a night of innocence lost. They will also tell you they have no doubt the perpetrator lived among them. He owned an '89 blue van, his name was Ronald Glen West, and his was the picture that Gord McAllister had pointed out.

For years after West's conviction for the Moorby/Ferguson murders, police work carried on in an attempt to establish West as the perpetrator of the egregious murders at this road stop on the Trans-Canada Highway. Evidence would be tirelessly re-examined, and countless tips followed up upon.

However, as Don MacNeil explained, "we couldn't get enough on West to give to the Crown—in fact, we were told that unless we could put West 'in' the motorhome [through trace evidence], there wasn't enough."

ॐ

My son Matt and I would visit the park during the research for this book, and we found it to be a particularly peaceful and beautiful spot, evoking fond memories of the north for both of us. We met a couple who had stopped at the site that day, both chatty and totally overwhelmed with the beauty of the little rest stop, perhaps reminiscent of what the McAllisters had felt some twenty-five years prior.

By the summer of 2018, Ed Pellarin was rapidly approaching his retirement date, but made no bones about the fact that he still wanted to close this enduring cold case.

The devil's paintbrush still blooms in Murder Park.

CHAPTER NINETEEN

The Model Prisoner

"There are certain crimes that are simply too cruel, too sadistic, too hideous to be forgiven."

—**John E. Douglas, FBI Profiler,** *Journey Into Darkness*

Following the Moorby/Ferguson murders, a profile was developed to assist in finding the killer. It was later proven to be largely off the mark, but this is not especially surprising, given that it was constructed during the infancy of profiling. Since the 1990s, profilers have become far more aware of the complexities in the development and character of a serial killer. Many preconceptions have been challenged. For example, by the 1970s, an increased number of murders were being committed by persons unknown to the victim, as people generally became more nomadic, given the increase in general access to transportation.

What goes into the making of a sexual sadistic criminal? Common theories include poverty, childhood abuse (sexual, physical, or psychological), violence in the media, pornography, genetics, insanity, premenstrual syndrome, and even blood sugar imbalance.

The list goes on and on, but experts will tell you that there is no single factor. "The most obvious and frightening reason," says legendary FBI profiler Roy Hazelwood, "is because they want to, and they like it, and they have no regard for what the rest of society thinks!"[3]

In recent times, the term psychopath has largely been replaced with "antisocial personality disorder" (APD). Such individuals feel no remorse or shame, guilt or appropriate fear. They do not learn from punishment, are easily bored, like excitement, and find it difficult to delay gratification, no matter where their self-interests may lie.

During the trial of America's most prolific serial killer, Gary Ridgway—dubbed the Green River Killer and known to be responsible for the murder of forty-eight women and suspected of closer to ninety—an illuminative moment occurred. During the victim impact statements, a father of one of the victims offered Ridgway his forgiveness. In a hushed courtroom, the father said that his faith compelled him to forgive. It was the only time Ridgway showed any emotion. He cried—but it was most likely for himself.

☙

Sexual sadists are almost invariably psychopaths and achieve their gratification not from sexual release but from the thrill of domination, control, and power. The crimes that they commit are given birth in fantasies which sometimes extend as far back as their early teens. These fantasies are often grandiose and can be described as a mental rehearsal of a desired event.[4]

The rehearsal plays a major role in the acting out of the fantasy, and in its perceived "success." Why did West commit a second murder so close on the heels of the first? Perhaps the murder of Doreen Moorby had been disappointing to West, with things not playing out as he had planned, and he remained fixated on fulfilling his fantasy: asserting power over a woman who substituted for the true subject of his anger. Maybe it was in this context that he encountered Helen Ferguson, who would have been easily visible to passers-by most days, as she waited with her daughter for the school bus.

There are generally considered two types of sexual sadistic offenders: compulsive and ritualistic. It would seem that West is likely the latter—all indications are that he most likely spent significant amounts of time working out the mechanics of his sexual offence.

It is thought all ritualistic offenders bring different individual perspectives to the crimes they commit.[5] Such perspectives are often relational: a fantasy between themselves and the victim, such as husband/wife, boyfriend/girlfriend, or consensual lovers, even though the victim is a stranger.[6] West's relationship with his mother was later well-established to be quite hostile. Was he expressing this anger by asserting power over someone else's mother? Both crimes occurred in familial rural settings, and some strong comparisons of appearance were made between West's mother and both victims.

Many angry and retaliatory sexual murderers commit their offences with the intent to kill the female victim during or after the activity. This is often driven by a deep-seated hatred of women, stemming from the resentment of a dominating female present in early life. The victim is often the surrogate for the original figure who caused the killer to feel emotionally invalidated.

It is possible West's victims were killed purely to eliminate them as witnesses (as West himself claimed), and that the murders were not necessarily part of fulfilling a fantasy. This might explain why he left the young boys alive. Regardless, the fact that he had no hesitation in ending the lives of their mothers should leave us horror-struck.

ॐ

Along with exhibiting the behaviour of a sexual sadist, it has been suggested West is also a narcissist and held a strong presumption of entitlement.[7] Strongly indifferent to the needs and feelings of others, narcissists often engage in high-risk activity, even though in every other aspect they are highly organized.

Narcissistic offenders are known to often keep journals and

mementos—or, as profiler Roy Hazelwood describes them, "work products."[8] These enable the offender to re-enact the crime in their imagination. West was to retain and squirrel away the ownership of his .22-calibre, 9-shot revolver. Was this his memento, his keepsake? Was this West's way of enjoying and reliving the crimes? Inspector Don MacNeil and his task force would come to be grateful for this potential aspect of West's narcissistic personality disorder.

Was it similarly narcissistic behaviour in the Sudbury pawn shop that caused West to be caught for the 1995 robberies? He had, after all, led a life of constant crime since his youth, and that hadn't stopped him from gaining enrollment into the Metro Toronto Police Force, devoid of suspicion. Other than a short period of incarceration for armed robbery in British Columbia in the mid-seventies, West had remained free to live as he wished, and quite possibly felt immune to discovery, something Roy Hazelwood refers to as the "bulletproof syndrome."[9]

In one study by Hazelwood, it was found that a significant number of sexual sadists were compulsive drivers, and that this was predominant among the more physically-violent offenders.[10] One subject said that "driving gave him a sense of freedom from responsibility." One of Hazelwood's students would suggest that driving provides the offender with constantly-changing visual stimulation, requiring little effort on his part. This desire for travel certainly seems to be reflected in West's far-spread robberies of the mid-nineties.

Additionally, many sexual sadists are "police buffs," and more than a few have worked in the field. Some have utilized their uniform to gain the victim's trust. It has been theorized West may have worn his uniform or flashed his badge when approaching Doreen or Helen or both; this potential strategy would further connect him to the killings at Murder Park, where the perpetrator had declared himself a police officer to the McAllisters.

West demonstrated himself to be a primarily organized offender. He would bring his preferred weapons: these were initially guns, but later, during the robberies, included a wrench, bindings, and a starter pistol. Organized killers also tend to hunt outside their own immediate neighbourhoods and remain relatively calm and controlled throughout the crime.

Organized killers are frequently interested in police techniques, and often closely follow their crimes through the media, even going so far as to find means to insert themselves into the investigation. There were some reports (in the post-sentencing media) that West may have helped to circulate the posters with the murderer's likeness back in 1970. Regardless of the veracity of this claim, West would have been in a position to access investigation information, and to use his acquired knowledge as a police officer to evade pursuit. He was likely aware that when chosen victims are random strangers, identification of the perpetrator becomes far more difficult.

℞

Sexual offenders are often said to be experiencing stress at the time of their attacks.[11] The stress may be relational, medical, financial, sexual, or caused by substance abuse. The rapist discovers the assault momentarily relieves stress and restores to them, if only temporarily, their personal sense of control and power. As Douglas expresses it, "most are angry, ineffectual losers who feel they've been given the shaft by life" and that "most of them have experienced some sort of physical or emotional abuse. Seldom would the subject direct his anger towards the focus of his resentment."[12]

Triggering stressors, such as the loss of a job, wife, or girlfriend, are often known to precede the crime. Only weeks prior to the 1970 murders, West and his brother Carl were known to have had a huge blow-up with their mother Phyllis, when she chose to have a man not much older than Ron move in with her. Both Doreen and Helen were not much younger than Phyllis, and the women, especially Helen, were said to bear a resemblance to her.

Carl West has stated their mother had been "particularly hard on Ron" as a child, but we also know Ron had abused Carl at length. Many profilers to this day struggle with whether criminals are either born or made.

One somewhat-controversial theory exists which demonstrates the high percentage of both mass murderers and serial killers who have suffered brain trauma. Was West speaking truthfully when he indicated the dent in his head to Reina, and credited it to his mother hitting him with a frying pan?

Additional similarities exist between West and other offenders. Between an extended illness and early death, West's father was mostly out of the picture while Ron was in his late teens. Acquaintances from West's youth confirmed he was not only abusive to his brother, but at least one other young boy, who was described by others to be "quiet and somewhat effeminate."

West was a suspected fire-starter and said to exhibit a stutter from time to time. I, among others, recall West's disdain for eye contact, especially so with women. A few of his youthful friends knew of the ease in which he would rob those who, "didn't take care of their belongings."

There is another possible—although unsubstantiated—similarity between West and other serial killers. It was generally rumoured West's mother was actually the daughter of a woman she grew up believing to be her sister, and that her actual grandparents were believed by her to be her parents. Both Ted Bundy and Aileen Wuornos (whose story was documented in the movie *Monster*) share a similar heritage. If this rumour was true, did West know about it?

᪥

One might wonder if West purposefully committed his crimes in two separate policing jurisdictions. In the 1970s, communications between forces were not fluid, and West may have known just how to take full advantage of this.

Geographic profiling or mapping was unheard of for investigative purposes prior to 1995. Dr. Kim Rossmo, a former Vancouver Police Department officer, first developed the concept.[13] Simply put, Rossmo established the potential locations of offenders based on the locations of the crimes. He developed a mathematical equation for the profiling, along with a software program known as Rigel. This program has been effectively incorporated to date by various Canadian agencies, as well as the FBI, Scotland Yard, and the Bureau of Alcohol, Tobacco, Firearms and Explosives.

The mapping concept demonstrates that criminals generally reserve a buffer zone close to home base and "would, like a person going shopping, favour locations that are convenient." This is thoroughly reflected in West's choice of crime scenes, which were not too close to home, but conveniently situated between his workplace and his residence, as well as en route to a place where he chose to vacation.

A killer's mental map will take into account all the things he needs: convenience, ease of access, and an escape route. West's home base in Scarborough would appear to sit well within the perimeters demonstrated by geographic profiling. The sites West chose were known to him, relatively rural and isolated, and there were multiple escape routes. There are a number of unsolved cold cases that also fit into West's mapping zone— these will be expounded upon in a later chapter addressing unsolved cold cases.

᪥

West was close to completing his eight-year term for the 1995 robberies when the OPP closed in on him for the Moorby/Ferguson murders. A detention review was conducted, during which it was noted: "You have recently been charged with two counts of murder in connection with the shooting deaths of two women in 1970. You have yet to be tried on these charges, and as yet, no bail has been set. The principles of the Board are specifically set out in Section 101 of the Corrections and Conditional Release Act. The first identified principle is that the protection of society is the paramount consideration in the determination of any case."

The review continued: "Of considerable concern to the Board is that despite your participation in treatment programming, and clinical support for a gradual release into the community, neither the program facilitators, nor the psychologist was aware of these new charges."

And so close to freedom. He had only just been considered for day parole at that time and determined as low-risk for further violence. More than one officer was to comment on West's apparent ability to present as a "model prisoner" and stay below the radar on the inside. He had, no doubt, been looking forward to release, and possibly to picking up where he left off.

It appears that when word got out amongst the inmate population regarding the nature of West's early crimes, he was warned to "leave the range." Within penitentiaries, there exists a lack of tolerance among the inmates for particular crimes, as well as for ex-police officers. Following an encounter with an inmate, West requested segregation. Rather than freedom, West would be looking to share a range with the likes of Paul Bernardo.

Given the nature of his sentencing for the 1970 murders, West became eligible for parole in 2011, but he does not appear to have applied then or since. Perhaps he too clearly recalls the resolve of the Ferguson family to show up at each and every hearing. Detective Constable John K. Smith speculates that West may choose to spend the rest of his days behind bars in relatively medium-to-low security.

On March 7, 2017, Ronald Glen West turned seventy years old. Expressing the dark humour which is often a common antidote for the impact of "dealing with the devil," Ed Pellarin and John K. Smith joked that perhaps they should drop in and wish a happy birthday to the model prisoner. Little did either of them realize that on the very same day, on the very same grounds, the former Colonel Russell Williams was celebrating his fifty-fourth birthday.

CHAPTER TWENTY

The Cold Corridor

"Where you used to be, there is a hole in the world, which I find myself constantly walking around in the daytime, and falling in at night. I miss you like hell."

—Edna St. Vincent Millay

It is accepted that the majority of outstanding Ontario-based cold cases occurred during two distinctive cycles: two five-year periods at the beginning of the 1970s and the 1980s. These two waves have been referred to as "The Killing Seasons."

In giving weight to the words of many personnel involved in one way or another with the Moorby and Ferguson murders, all expressing the belief that "there have to be more," it may be prudent to address a number of cases that have remained cold. In no way am I suggesting West is specifically considered a suspect in any of the following, but instead that considering him in respect to these cases proves for an interesting examination of geographic profiling.

Most occurred within the corridor of West's activity during the period of time he served with Metro Toronto Police Division 53, from 1966 to 1972. The cases included here were generally initiated or culminated within the Oak Ridges Moraine and the triangle established between: West's apartment in Scarborough, his holiday site in the Musselman Lake area, and his family home in Amaranth.

CATHY AND LEE

On October 1, 1971, an unusually warm Friday evening, thirteen-year-old Catherine (Cathy) Potter and fifteen-year-old Lee Kirk left the group home (on Rochelle Court in North York) where they both resided to visit Lee's biological father, who resided in Richmond Hill. Both girls were wards of the Children's Aid Society and shared the home of Mr. and Mrs. Robert McMaster with four other youngsters. After supper, the girls were given a ride by Mr. McMaster to a bus stop at the corner of Yonge Street and Finch Avenue, and had promised to return that evening by 11 p.m.

When the girls, who were considered reliable, did not return by 11 p.m., the police were called. There had been an elevated number of robberies, beatings, and sexual assaults in the area. (In fact, 1971 had seen the estimated number of rapes in Toronto increase by 10 percent over the previous year.) An extensive search followed, but with no sign of either girl.

Pickering Township's Valley Farm Road and gravel pit proved a popular spot with teens at the time, ostensibly as a place to hang out, drink, and ride motorcycles and dune-buggies. On October 3, two young boys cutting through the gravel pit discovered the bodies of the two young women, which were side-by-side and partially concealed by some sumac bushes. The boys reportedly saw blood on the nearby grass and on an abandoned cement block. Police, upon investigation, felt both girls had been killed somewhere else and dumped at the pit.

Both girls were fully dressed, with no obvious signs of sexual assault. One of the girls was particularly badly beaten, and both had died due to strangulation by ligature. They were both estimated to have died around 9:30 p.m. on the evening of their disappearance.

An aspect of the scene that may have seemed encouraging to the investigative officers was that on the clothes of both girls were found multiple flakes of paint in numerous colours that were typically used on motorcycles or customized cars. Both of the girls' shoes and clothes exhibited traces of items that could be found on the floor of an auto body shop, and there were indications that both girls had been in an upright position when the beatings occurred.

Police scoured multiple body shops to no avail, and even though there were hundreds of tips at the time, they were unable to progress closer to solving the double homicide. The only consistent lead was that a dark, late-model car had been seen near the dumping site. It was believed the girls most likely spent their bus fare on cigarettes and opted to hitch-hike that fateful evening.

The body shop evidence led the police to consider motorcycle gang involvement, but they were unable to establish a connection. Additionally, this would not explain how the girls had most likely been picked up in, and dumped from, a car.

West had operated a police motorcycle at Metro for a brief time, which might suggest the possible transference of body shop evidence. It would appear that sexual assault was not the prime motive in this particular case, but there was an indication of excessive anger and violence, which may have occurred to assure neither of the girls could survive to act as witnesses and identify their attacker. Lastly, the area in Pickering where the girls' bodies were found was not far from West's home in nearby Scarborough.

INGRID

Ingrid Bauer was fourteen in the summer of 1972. She was blonde, rather striking, a good student, got along well with her family, and was even taking some modelling courses.

Ingrid's father, Oscar, who worked for Kodak in Toronto, had driven to the family cottage in Thornbury on Friday, August 11. Ingrid, her mother and little brother Kevin had been there since the end of July. The next few days proved wet and rainy, so Oscar planned to head back home on the sixteenth when Ingrid decided to join him, leaving Mrs. Bauer and Kevin behind.

Upon returning to the family home in Kleinburg, Ingrid decided to surprise her boyfriend, Larry Teeple, also fourteen, who lived about eight kilometres to the south in Woodbridge. There was no public transportation at this time as Kleinburg and the surrounding area were still relatively rural. At 9:30 p.m. Ingrid set out barefoot, planning on walking or perhaps even hitching a ride with a local. In this era, children were not necessarily discouraged from hitchhiking, but warned only to be discerning. Rides were often offered by known friends and neighbours in small communities. Ingrid promised her father she would return by 10:30 p.m.

Ingrid's older brother, Brent, was already at home when his sister and father returned from the cottage, and he left shortly after Ingrid to buy cigarettes at the corner store. Brent saw Ingrid waiting for a ride at the corner of Islington Avenue and Pennon Road, noting a police cruiser near the same intersection.

When he exited the store, Brent noticed Ingrid was no longer there, and he returned home. An additional sighting of Ingrid was reported by eighteen-year-old Terry Bell, who said he saw Ingrid heading south on Islington at about 9:45 p.m.

A little while after Brent returned home, Ingrid's boyfriend Larry called to ask where Ingrid was. Oscar and Brent immediately started a search, heading towards Larry's home in Woodbridge, checking ditches as they drove, allowing for the possibility that she may have been hit by a passing car. But there was no sign of Ingrid. Upon returning home, Oscar called the police, assuring them Ingrid was a responsible girl. The police immediately commenced a search.

An area of over twenty square miles was scoured by over

two hundred individuals. Police, firemen, and volunteers all participated, hopeful of finding a live, pretty, five-foot-six and one-hundred-pound girl with flowing blonde hair and laughing brown eyes. Hesitantly, searches in and around the Humber River were also conducted.

But Ingrid had disappeared without a trace.

Soon after, several witnesses came forward to say they had heard the "cries of a young person" and had noticed an unidentified pickup truck in the area of Islington and Sevilla Drive.

Fourteen hundred leads came in, with supposed sightings of Ingrid across both Canada and America. There were forty-four sightings in all, and police painstakingly followed up on every single one. This massive search was Ontario's most publicized to date.

Oscar would pay for billboards in thirteen Canadian cities, and he manned the ever-ringing home phone as tips came in. He blamed himself for Ingrid's disappearance—he should have driven her that evening. The German immigrant would die at eighty-seven, only months after attending the Newmarket Courthouse to declare that his beloved Ingrid was undoubtedly deceased.

This appeared to be a crime of opportunity. Other than time and geography, the main factor that connects West is Brent's sighting of a police car at the corner where Ingrid waited for a time, hoping for a ride. It was Kleinburg and not Toronto, but it is conceivable West could have been in the area. What colour was the cruiser Brent saw? Had it been black and white? Metro Toronto cruisers at the time were a distinctive yellow.

No sign of Ingrid was ever found, which suggests she was moved a considerable distance by someone becoming skilled in having their victims disappear.

Ingrid's disappearance occurred one month prior to West leaving the force for good.

YVONNE

As a youngster, Yvonne Leroux's parents described her as "indus-trious, smart, a little too independent, and brave." Yvonne's short life played out as a true tragedy. In 1971, at the age of fifteen, Yvonne reported being raped by four boys. Charges were laid, only to be dropped five months later. Shortly after, Yvonne—along with the dog she had rescued as a puppy and raised—ran away from her Finch and Keele home.

Her family followed up on sightings of Yvonne for months, some of them as far away as Windsor, but to no avail. Nine months later, Yvonne returned with three tattooed dots in the shape of a triangle on the web of the skin between the thumb and the index finger on both of her hands. This tattoo has often been associated with gangs, and Yvonne's family believed it signified Yvonne was now property of the motorcycle gang she had described getting mixed up with.

Yvonne never revealed to her family which gang it was, but said she had told the gang she would not become a drug runner for them. She expressed to her family they could be in danger if she told them too much. Yvonne also insisted that "the police and the gang were very tight."

In spite of everything, she began to put her life back togeth-er, attending school, finding a part-time job, and going to coun-selling. She expressed fear of the gang members, and it appeared she was living under a very real threat. Yvonne's mother, Diana, taxied her everywhere, rarely letting Yvonne out of her sight.

About a month before Yvonne went missing, she was fright-ened by an incident which occurred as she left a local event, running back inside and exclaiming, "Oh my God, they are out there, they want to kill me!" Members of the family felt they were being watched, and a neighbour said he had repeatedly seen a car sitting outside their home.

On Friday, November 29, 1972, Yvonne attended her coun-selling session near the York Finch Hospital at Oakdale Road.

Her mother arrived to pick her up after the session, and when she didn't see Yvonne waiting at the door, she ran inside, only to be told Yvonne had left just moments before.

Yvonne's body was found the next day in King Township, at the Sixteenth Sideroad between Jane and Keele, not that far west of Gormley. Yvonne had died due to blunt force trauma to the back of the head, and it appeared as though her body had been dumped off where it was found.

Purportedly, there was male DNA recovered at the murder site. Inquiries by York Regional Police, with the Centre for Forensic Sciences, were reported as having been made as recently as 2016, but with no results yet divulged. West's DNA profile is in the system.

JANICE

There is little information regarding the life and death of twenty-two-year-old Janice Montgomery. She was murdered in November of 1972. Police believed she had been hitchhiking when she was taken to a lonely field in Georgetown and shot in the back of the head with a small calibre revolver. The perpetrator had removed all the labels from her clothes before leaving her body propped up against a tree. No cartridges were left behind.

Janice does not appear to be listed in any of the OPP's cold case files at this time. It would seem her killer was well aware of police procedure in determining the identity of homicide victims.

ISABELLE

The sweet and smiling face of sixty-eight-year-old Isabella Brooks continues to sit atop the short paragraph that documents her disappearance in the York Regional Police cold case files. Isabelle and her husband Aubrey lived in a small house on a property at the southwest corner of Highway 7 and Tenth Concession (now Reesor Road) on the east side of Markham.

According to Aubrey, on the evening of Saturday, March 4, 1972, Isabelle left the home on foot and told him she would return in one week. She was wearing her glasses, a black or maroon coat, and a headscarf. She was never seen again.

Little information remains regarding Isabelle's departure. It appears that Aubrey believed she was going to her sister's. This may not have been unusual, but we don't know where that was or how she planned to get there. We don't know if she had any luggage or might have been catching a bus (or some other mode of transportation), or how cold it was. Geography and the time period may be the only factors that connect West.

ॐ

There were at least two more unsolved murders of young women in the area during the first half of the 1970s before the trend slowed. By this time, Ron West was accumulating charges and serving time for armed robbery in British Columbia.

In the following decades, he also spent a lot of time in the vast reaches of Northern Ontario, travelling widely there, proximate to much of the province's Indigenous population. (Ron's wife, Barbara, was Ojibwe.) Therefore, let us not neglect to mention the thousands of cold cases that make up Canada's national crisis: Missing and Murdered Indigenous Women. If West was looking for potential victims, he may very well have been drawn to the socially and economically marginalized.

Ron West has only been convicted of two murders. "There have to be more."

Consider the conviction of Don Hillock: "I worked on that case until I was raw. I cannot and I will never believe that he did not kill more people. You don't just kill two people, and enjoy it, and then not kill anybody for years. That's been bugging me for forty-seven years. I just can't believe he didn't do more. I've always had a problem with that, always!"

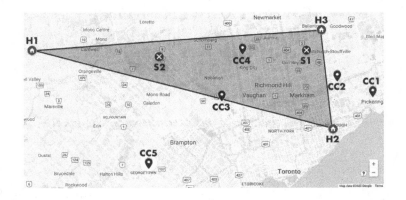

—Geographic Profile of Ron West from 1966 to 1972.
(Google Map by Jennifer Bennett and Ann Burke)

West's Regular Destinations
H1—West farm, 10th Line of Amaranth in Dufferin County
H2—West home, Painted Post Drive, Scarborough, Toronto
H3—West camping area, Musselman's Lake

1970 Murder Sites
S1—Doreen's home, Bethesda Side Road, Gormley
S2—Helen's home, Highway 50, Palgrave

Cold Cases
CC1—Cathy and Lee, Valley Farm Road, Pickering
CC2—Isabelle, Reesor Road, Markham
CC3—Ingrid, Islington Avenue, Kleinburg
CC4—Yvonne, 16th Sideroad, King Township
CC5—Janice, Georgetown field

CHAPTER TWENTY-ONE

Afterwards

"In life, unlike chess, the game continues after checkmate."
—Isaac Asimov

In 2001, Donald J. MacNeil spent his last day on the job doing a ride-along with his son Michael, who was serving with Barrie Police Services at the time. Permission had been given by the one and same Wayne Frechette, former polygrapher in the Moorby/ Ferguson investigation and then-acting chief of Barrie Police Services. Michael would eventually join the OPP, but not until after his dad's retirement. "It was hard to work in the shadow of someone bigger than life," said Michael. "Everybody knew him."

Don was known by various nicknames over the course of his career: the Old Dog, the Old War Horse, and of course he also consisted as one half of the Gold Dust Twins, along with Floyd Stewart. Floyd has also since retired, settling back into his home province of Prince Edward Island, returning occasionally to Ontario and dropping in on Don. They continue to toast "to the good times, the bad times, and the Maritimes" on every anniversary of the day they joined the OPP.

Don no longer passes the time bobbing up and down on Lake Couchiching aboard his little sailboat without a name. He has, however, remained very active since his retirement, serving for over five years on the Orillia Police Services Board, as well as monitoring security for a local women's shelter. Until recently, Don, widowed since May of 2007, wintered in Florida each year, with a few side trips to Las Vegas.

One of Don's most prized achievements during his policing career was serving as president from 1996 to 1997 for the Harvard Associates in Police Science, a group of both Canadian and American homicide investigators from the eastern seaboard of North America. He hosted the forty-ninth conference in the "Sunshine City" of Orillia during his presidency.

Don also took on the task of hosting the annual International Conference for Homicide Investigation—again in Orillia. The conference included such notables as Donna French, the mother of Kristen French, who was murdered by Paul Bernardo and then-wife Karla Homolka. Donna has become a strong advocate for victims' rights.

—**OPP Commissioner Tom O'Grady (left) and
Detective Inspector Don J. MacNeil (right).
(Kindly made available by OPP Museum)**

Over the last several years, since our first memorable meeting in the Mariposa Market in Orillia, Don and I have become friends, and I have discovered that, in spite of his dour presence, he can be bought over for no less than a few homemade blueberry muffins. We have spent many hours in Don's cozy living room, surrounded by masses of John Wayne pictures, books, and paraphernalia—Don definitely has a fixation on the Duke. I once told Don's son Michael his father reminded me of some of the characters Wayne played. For me, Don epitomizes real-life "true grit."

A picture of Don's "boat with no name" hangs on one of the condo walls, the same boat where Don sat when he learned Ronald Glen West had copped a guilty plea. In a sitting room off the living room, is a picture of Blue, the dog Don claims was smarter than some cops he knew. Blue was actually his son Mike's dog, but Don made no bones about coveting the dog. "That dog could find anything, no matter how well it was hidden." Don recalled a story of Blue once finding a football in a snow drift. I wondered if this might be a case of Don subconsciously relating to traits of his own.

There are commendations, laminated newspaper accounts, certificates, photographs, and more, all reflecting a historic career. In 2017, several of Don's fellow officers and friends joined him to celebrate his seventy-fifth birthday. I don't believe anything could have pleased him more.

ॐ

Detective Sergeant Ed Pellarin, originally scheduled to retire from the Ontario Provincial Police by November of 2017, chose to stay on for the meantime. "We have one more daughter to put through school," he stated. His three girls have all but fled the nest. They seem mostly set on careers in health care, just like their mother.

Ed is one of what would appear to be a small number of OPP officers to have served their entire career in one location—

in Ed's case, Blind River. Not only is it unusual for an officer to spend his entire career working in the same community, but also to live within its midst and be held in such high regard is truly unique and commendable. Both Frank and Kenny Kennedy of the Riverside Tavern spoke of Ed in nothing but glowing terms—also recalling how he had once won a barbecue in a draw held at the Tavern. Mel Hall, the widow of Ed's early roommate Andrew, also extolled the "gentle bear" that Ed epitomizes.

I asked Ed what he planned to do when he retired and he told me he thinks he would like to do some landscaping, and of course some fishing. Ed has an obvious affinity for living close to nature in his beloved Northern Ontario.

Ed also expressed a continued desire to one day prove who was responsible for the ghastly Murder Park slaughter. There appears to be no doubt in Ed's mind as to who the lone gunman was on that summer night in 1991, but the case remains cold in the courts to this day.

—York Regional Police Chief Don Hillock.
(Courtesy of Joan Hillock)

~

Many of the officers involved in the Moorby/Ferguson murder cases were to rise considerably high through the ranks. Don Hillock ultimately served as Chief of Police for York Region, but the memory of the two murders never strayed far: "That case is embedded in my memory. It's not something that comes and goes. I can remember almost everything about that case."

It would, however, not be the only case that would haunt Hillock. He had always hoped he could solve the disappearance of little Cheryl Anne Hanson. The pretty seven-year-old had left her Aurora home one May evening in 1974, never to be seen again. Thousands of volunteers searched for her, including police, but to no avail. Convicted murderer Donald Everingham confessed to several additional murders, including that of Cheryl Anne, but even after Everingham led the police to where he said he had left the murdered child, the body was never found. Everingham's confession was eventually refuted.

Upon retirement, Don Hillock and his wife Joan would split time between their home in Orangeville (where we met for the first time) and their cottage in Gravenhurst. It was only by sheer luck that I had eventually connected with him. Initially, I'd had little luck getting in touch, and was near giving up when I called the York info line and found myself speaking with a good friend of Don and his family. She, in turn, called Don, and he telephoned me the next day—he definitely wanted to talk about the West case!

For our second visit, I travelled to Don and Joan's cottage in Gravenhurst in the summer of 2017. Don was never more content than here. A large shed/woodshop had been erected near the actual cottage, decorated with a street sign indicating "Don Hillock Drive." Don spent hours carving wooden birds, which Joan would patiently hand paint. Don also delved in a unique form of taxidermy on what he described as "roadkill": animals who had died from natural causes.

After many happy years of retirement, Don's health started to fail, and in late 2017 he was given up to a year to live. After my suggestion that Don record his remarkable life, he frantically began putting his memoirs together to present to his family, hoping to finish by the summer of 2018.

Sadly, Don Hillock was to pass away in his sleep on March 22, 2018, the day before what would have been his seventy-seventh birthday. Don's beloved "Joanie" continued with the work of compiling Don's life story—there for Don as always.

Don would have been pleased to see the incredible show of respect by York Regional Police at his memorial service in Orangeville on April 7, 2018. I smiled inwardly when I saw two of his carved mallards at the rear of the hall, but I was relieved to see that the "roadkill" taxidermy pieces had not made an appearance.

ॐ

Max Haines passed away at age eighty-six on September 30, 2017, after a relatively long battle with progressive supranuclear palsy, an incurable neurological disorder not unlike Parkinson's disease. I spoke with Max's wife Marilyn just prior to his passing, and we chatted about Max's long-time obsession with the unsolved Moraine murders. It was a case he resurrected regularly in his newspaper columns, right up until the day Don MacNeil called him to happily report: "We've got him, Max, we've got him!

After Max passed away, I called Marilyn and was startled to hear the answering machine spout, in Max's unmistakable voice, "You have reached Max and Marilyn, we cannot take your call right now, please leave a message ..." I would later discover Marilyn was not the only widow to keep memories alive this way. It also reminded me of how my daughter found comfort in calling her late Grandma's number before it was taken down, just to hear her voice once more, even if it was only a recording.

Wayne Frechette retired from the OPP after forty years with the rank of detective chief superintendent—only to sign on as police chief for the City of Barrie, Ontario, serving from 2001 to 2010. Here our lives were destined to cross once again: during Wayne's tenure as police chief, he secured mental health awareness training for his force. This was particularly important to me, as at that time I was serving as coordinator for the David Busby Street Centre in Barrie, where over 80 percent of our clients suffered from a variety of mental health issues.

Wayne, now fully retired, splits his time between his home in Innisfil, Ontario, and his cottage near Algonquin Park. He is always up for a round of golf.

Gord Wauchope, who went to high school with West, played hockey with West, and served as a Metropolitan Toronto Police officer with West, also later served as the mayor of Innisfil, Ontario.

Keith Rogers—the Toronto cop whose meticulously maintained notebooks helped crack the West case—is now fully retired after spending a number of years in private investigation.

Detective Corporal John K. Smith continues to serve with the Ontario Provincial Police. He went on to work in witness protection and on cases that dealt with child pornography. John's children were quite taken aback when they one day uncovered a front-page newspaper picture of their father escorting Ronald Glen West from the courthouse after his conviction. John doesn't generally talk about his work with his family. When reflecting on John's inquiry of West, and how Ron could leave two little boys without their mother, one is not surprised.

Larry Matkowski, former brother-in-law to Ron's brother Carl, left the OPP but continues to work as a special constable for Mono Township in Dufferin County. He still wonders whatever became of Carl, who remains missing to this day.

Reina LaCroix, the trusting soul whose life was torn apart by West, passed away on October 11, 2015. She would be recalled in her obituary as having a "tremendous love of animals" and was known to many as the "Martha Stewart of Blind River."

Barbara Nayotchekeesic, Ronald West's wife and the mother of his two sons, has retreated into private life in Northern Ontario. Her sons are heard to be living productive and blameless lives. The extent of the abuse they experienced is not known.

Helen Ferguson's mother, Jean Martindale, passed away in 2010 at the age of 103. In 2011, the Helen Ferguson Nursing Education Award was established by Helen's family in her memory. It was designed to provide funding support towards continuing education for registered nurses, in order to enhance their ability to provide comprehensive, holistic, quality care to patients and their families.

Those who considered themselves friends of West's in his youth continue to struggle with the enormity of it all. Gazing across the beautiful rolling Mulmur Hills where he now resides, not far from the Amaranth of his youth, with an old high school yearbook in his lap, Carl Alexander reflects that "I may think more about Ron than anyone does these days, as I try to somehow equate who he was with what he became."

I recently reconnected with Lois Metz, the youth worker at the Honeywood Rural Learning Centre with whom I shared that life-changing day in September of 1992. Afterwards, I thought to myself how little we talked about that day, and the case that started all of this for me ... instead, we talked about those we loved and how fortunate we were.

CHAPTER TWENTY-TWO

Letters to the Devil

"We have never heard the devil's side of the story,
God wrote all the book."

—Anatole France

When I began to research and record the events of West's crimes, I never thought about where the sometimes-disturbing road I had taken would lead me. Perhaps nothing leading up to this moment in my life had yet demanded that I fulfill what ultimately became so obvious. Could I ask the questions that remained?

It didn't seem enough to just recount all that had occurred to date, demonstrating how others had so effectively put the pieces of the puzzle into place. There remained unanswered questions, along with victims who endured unspoken pain, continuing to wait and yearn for answers during their lifetime. Could I ask West those questions? Would he allow me to?

During one of my early meetings with Detective Sergeant Ed Pellerin, we discussed whether I had considered writing to West. I said I hadn't. "Why wouldn't you?" Ed asked me. And there it was.

I knew that I must, and after much thought and consideration, I did.

I wrote the first letter to West in May of 2017, largely on the premise of needing his permission to see the RCMP records pertaining to his incarceration in British Columbia in the mid-seventies. I had been informed I would need West's signed approval to gain the records under the Freedom of Information Act. To this request, I added the question of his thoughts on me attending the Bath Institute in Millhaven to meet with him one-on-one, reminding him that many years ago we were once high school classmates.

After dropping the letter in the mailbox, I would spend countless hours posing questions to an imaginary "older" version of the high school boy I now only barely recalled. I would also often be surprised and confused by the unsummoned image of sheets blowing in the wind on a clothesline—doubtless Doreen's. How I would manage a one-on-one with West became a dominating, frightening, and even consuming thought.

The months went by and I heard nothing in return.

By November of 2017, still having heard nothing, I discarded the premise of asking permission for the viewing of records, and, in a second letter, I flat out asked West for the opportunity to meet at the prison. I wanted to hear from him directly. I wanted to hear his story.

I spent hours poring over everything I could find that might assist me in gaining the confidence of a known narcissistic sexual psychopath. I knew West had refused all requests for meetings in the past. I felt I too would most likely become another rejected visitor.

I told West I was writing a book about him and wanted him to have the opportunity to see that I got it "right." It made me feel rather sick to my stomach, this pandering to his ego, but I held on to my underlying motive. I wanted an opportunity to see if he would talk about Murder Park.

I had heard West might be planning to spend the rest of his life incarcerated. Was there anyone on the outside who would care for, or about, this aging murderer? West had not applied for parole to date, even though eligible. I hoped beyond hope he might be ready to talk about his long-suspected role in the Blind River murders. It was worth the attempt, as I knew family members of the victims continued to wait for the day when they might hear who was responsible for taking the lives of those they loved. West had once hinted to Ed Pellerin he just might be prepared to discuss Murder Park one day.

I cannot presume to know what allowances the law may make to secure a confession. There is an understandable desperation to secure closure for the victims' families, and yet we remember all too well the contentious "cash for bodies" deal made with Clifford Olson, the "Beast of B.C."

However, I knew all too well that West was likely to carry the details to his death, especially if he coveted his incarceration in a medium-to-low security institute. He might not be prepared to suffer the judgment of others who would no doubt hear of his additional crimes. He had asked to be moved within the penitentiary for his own protection years before, back when he was primarily surrounded by criminals convicted of the lesser charges of theft and assault. When those inmates learned of his pending murder charges, it was made apparent they felt him not worthy to be amongst mere armed thieves.

I recalled from my days of working with the homeless that, for some, incarceration was often preferable to the hunger and cold of living on the street, especially in advancing years. Would West really want to risk the likelihood of returning to the range? I had heard that by now even Paul Bernardo might be considered for a move to the less-constrictive realm of Bath Institute.

Bath Institute is located just east of Bath, Ontario, twenty-five kilometres west of Kingston. It is a stand-alone, medium-security facility based on an open campus design. Approximately 23 percent of Bath inmates are serving life, while the balance will most likely eventually be released. The population is made up of hardened criminals, including murderers, serial rapists, pedophiles with multiple convictions, and those serving longer sentences. The inmates live in dorm-like settings and nearly all take part in some form of work: there are kitchen workers, cleaners, caregivers to the older inmates, and wood-workers at the onsite factory that manufactures, among other things, office furniture for the Ministry of Defence. Inmates are required to attend extensive rehab programs up to five times a week.

I wasn't sure if West had stayed in contact with anyone on the outside, including family or old friends—or at least I had not found anyone who would admit that was the case. Most old friends and family expressed the desire to maintain as great a distance as possible between him and themselves.

I contacted Detective Sergeant Ed Pellarin, who was now on the verge of retirement, to let him know he had been instrumental in giving me the idea of approaching West in the first place.

Ed responded quickly, expressing that he still hoped to hear from West about what had been hinted at when he suggested to Ed that "we talk about [the Murder Park cases] one day." Ed asked me what I thought of us both meeting with West, and said he would seek his current superior's approval. I had to admit I felt relieved at the thought of Ed attending with me.

I never doubted for a moment that West was clever—I knew that to believe I could trick him into giving information was naive—but I had also learned that to guess at what a psychopath may choose to do was also naive.

Ed and I soon spoke again. After giving it some thought, he was concerned attending with me at this time might actually interfere with my plans.

I made the decision that should West agree to meet with me, prior to going to the Bath Institute I would arrange to see someone skilled and practiced in dealing with the psychopathic mind. It was worth a shot at a gaze into the abyss.

This story is not over.

ENDNOTES

1. Constable Carol Sobel, History of Policing in York Region, York Regional Police, Newmarket, Pg. 46
2. Charles Foran, Toronto Life Magazine, March 2002
3. Roy Hazelwood and Stephen G. Michaud, Dark Dreams, St. Martins, Pg. 15
4. Dark Dreams, Hazelwood/Michaud, Pg.19
5. Dark Dreams, Hazelwood/Michaud, Pg.43
6. Dark Dreams, Hazelwood/Michaud, Pg. 44
7. Dark Dreams, Hazelwood/Michaud, Pg. 63
8. Dark Dreams, Hazelwood/Michaud, Pg. 69
9. Dark Dreams, Hazelwood/Michaud, Pg. 72
10. Dark Dreams, Hazelwood/Michaud, Pg. 99
11. Mindhunter, John Douglas & Mark Olshaker, Gallery Books, 1995, Pg. 142
12. Mindhunter, Douglas/Olshaker, Pg. 111
13. Mapping the Trail of a Crime, Gordon Kerr, Amber Books, 2012

ABOUT THE AUTHOR

Photo Credit: Jenn Kanstein, Four Eyes Creative

After serving in the Royal Canadian Navy as a navigational operator/radar technician, Ann turned her interest to her greatest love, writing. Working largely in the social services sector as a counsellor in a women and children's shelter, coordinating a homeless drop-in, and directing a rural community centre, she freelanced for newspapers, including the *Toronto Star*. Her most memorable years were spent working for the *Walden Observer* in Lively, Ontario and covering events for the *Sudbury Star*.

She now lives in Innisfil with her husband.

www.annburkeauthor.com